OXFORD

Edward Thomas was born in 1879 and was killed at Arras in 1917.

In the years before the First World War he established a considerable reputation as a prose writer with a strong interest in the countryside and in the tradition of English letters. Among his best known works are *The Icknield Way*, *In Pursuit of Spring*, *Richard Jefferies*, *The Heart of England*, *The Woodland Life* and *Oxford*. His poetry, for which he is today best known, matured during the war and Thomas is now regarded as among the finest poets of his generation.

TOM TOWER, CHRIST CHURCH   FRED RICHARDS, R.E.

OXFORD

Edward Thomas

Hutchinson

London Melbourne Sydney Auckland Johannesburg

Hutchinson & Co. (Publishers) Ltd

An imprint of the Hutchinson Publishing Group

17-21 Conway Street, London WIP 6JD

Hutchinson Group (Australia) Pty Ltd
30-32 Cremorne Street, Richmond South, Victoria 3121
PO Box 151, Broadway, New South Wales 2007

Hutchinson Group (NZ) Ltd
32-34 View Road, PO Box 40-086, Glenfield, Auckland 10

Hutchinson Group (SA) Pty Ltd
PO Box 337, Bergvlei 2012, South Africa

First published 1903
Published as a Hutchinson Paperback 1983

Printed in Great Britain by The Anchor Press Ltd
and bound by Wm Brendon & Son Ltd,
both of Tiptree, Essex

British Library Cataloguing in Publication Data
Thomas, Edward
    Oxford
    1. Oxford (Oxfordshire) – Description – Guidebooks
    I. Title
    914.25'7404858   DA690.O98

ISBN 0 09 151721 4

Prefatory Note

Most of these chapters have been filled by a brief search into my recollections of Oxford. They aim, therefore, at recording my own impressions as faithfully as the resultant stir of fancy would allow. But I am also deeply and obviously indebted to several books, and in particular to the histories of Oxford by Parker, Maxwell Lyte, and Boase; to Mr. F. E. Robinson's series of College Histories; to *Reminiscences of Oxford* and its companion volumes from the Clarendon Press; and, above all the rest, to Anthony à Wood, and to the Rev. Andrew Clark's perfect editions of that writer's *Life and Times*, and of John Aubrey's *Brief Lives*. The Editors of *The Daily Chronicle*, *The Illustrated London News*, and *Crampton's Magazine* have kindly given me permission to reprint a few pages from my contributions thereto.

EDWARD THOMAS

Contents

ON ENTERING OXFORD

CHAPTER I

PASSING rapidly through London, with its roar of causes that have been won, and the suburbs, where they have no causes, and skirting the willowy Thames, —glassy or silver, or with engrailed grey waves —and brown ploughlands, elm-guarded, solitary, I approached Oxford. Nuneham woods made one great shadow on the land, one great shadow on the Thames. According to an old custom, it rained. But rain takes away nothing from Oxford save a few nice foot passengers. It transmutes the Franciscan habit of the city to a more Dominican cast ; and if the foil of sky be faintly lighted, the rain becomes a visible beatitude.

One by one the churches of St. Mary the Virgin and All Saints', and the pleasant spire of the Cathedral, appear ; with the dome of the Radcliffe Camera, Tom Tower of Christ Church, and that old bucolic tower of Robert d'Oigli's castle on the west. For a minute several haystacks, a gasometer, and the engine smoke replace them. But already that one cameo from

3

Oxford

February's hand has painted and lit and garnished again that city within the heart, which is Oxford. I think, when I see an old woodcut of a patron holding his towered foundation in his hand, about to bestow it as a gift,—as William of Wykeham is depicted, holding Winchester,—that even so Oxford gives to us the stones of church and college, the lawns and shrubs of gardens, and the waters of Isis, to be stored in the chambers of the soul—" Mother of Arts ! "

> Mother of arts
> And eloquence, native to famous wits
> Or hospitable, in her sweet recess
> City or suburban, studious walks and shades.

So ran my thoughts and Milton's verse ; and possessed, as it is easy to become in such a place, with its great beauty, thinking of its great renown, my mind went naturally on in the channel of that same stream of verse, while I saw the Christ Church groves, the Hinksey Hills, and the grey Isis—

> See there the olive grove of Academe,
> Plato's retirement, where the Attic bird
> Trills her thick-warbled notes the Summer long ;
> There, flowery hill, Hymettus, with the sound
> Of bees' industrious murmur, oft invites
> To studious musing ; there Ilissus rolls
> His whispering stream.

But the dark entry to the city, on the western side, suddenly changed my thoughts. It is well known. It is the most contemptible in Europe. It consists of a hoarding, a brewery, and suitable appurtenances. Of more recent date is the magnificent marmalade shop,

4

the most conspicuous building in Oxford. On the north and east the approach is not worse, consisting, as it does, of sermons in brick, arranged in perfectly successful imitation of Tooting. On the south the fields are melancholy in apprehension of a similar fate. In short, one ignorant of the city might believe that he was approaching the hub of the universe.

Then, the Norman tower appeared again, and the afforested castle mound rose up. A bell, and many bells, began to sound. The present vanished in charge of a westward-going motor car, containing three gentlemen with cigars and a lady; and the past, softer than the cooing of doves and more compelling than organ music, came with the twilight from the tower of St. Michael's church.

At sunset or at dawn the city's place in the world, as a beautiful thing, is clearest. Few cities look other than sad at those hours; many, unless hid in their own smoke, look cheap. Oxford becomes part of the magic of sunset and dawn,—is, as it were, gathered into the bosom of the power that is abroad. Yet, if it is one with the hills and the clouds and the silence, the human dignity of the place is also significant. The work of the ancient architect conspires with that of the sunset and of long, pregnant tracts of time; and I know not whether to thank, for the beauty of the place, its genius or perhaps the divinest series of accidents that have ever agreed to foster the forward-looking designs of men. In the days when what is admirable in Oxford was built, the builder made no pretence to please his neighbour. He made what he loved. In many cases he was probably indifferent to everything else. But the genius of the place took care ; and only the recent architects who have endeavoured to work in harmony with the place have failed. There is a gentle and puissant harmonising influence in Oxford which nothing can escape. I am no lover of Georgian architecture and am often blind to the power of Wren ; but in Oxford I have no such incapacities ; and I believe that here architecture should be judged, not as Norman or classical, as the work of Wolsey or Aldrich, but as Oxford architecture. The library at Christ Church, or any other work of the eighteenth century, seems to me as divine a thing, though as yet it lacks the complete unction of antiquity, as Mob Quad at Merton or Magdalen Tower. To pass from the Norman work of St. Peter's in the East to the Palladianism of Peckwater quadrangle, is but to descend from one to another of the same honourable race. If certain extremely new edifices wear out a thousand years they will probably be worthy of reverence at the end of that time, and be in harmony with Merton chapel and Balliol hall at once. Nothing is so deserving, few things so exacting, of respect, from transitory men as age. Things change, and improvements are questioned or questionable ; but, for me, age is as good as an improvement ; and Oxford honours what is old with particular dignities and graces ; under her influence the work of age is at once blander and more swift.

But this gentle tyranny,—as of the Mother of

On Entering Oxford

Christ, who, in Leonardo's picture, unites angel and holy child and St. John with outspread hands,— is exerted not only upon the stones, but also upon the people of the place. A man may at Oxford rejoice in the company of another whom it is a self-sacrifice to meet elsewhere. He finds himself marvelling that one who was merely a gentleman in London can be interesting in Long Wall Street or on the Cherwell. The superb, expensive young man who thinks that there is " practically nobody in Oxford "— the poor, soiled scholar—the exuberant, crimson-lipped athlete, whose stride is a challenge, his voice a trumpet call—the lean and larded æsthete, busily engaged upon the quaint designs of oriental life,—all discover some point in common when they are seen together in the Schools, or on the riverside.

I was never more effectually reminded of this Oxford magic than when I heard the City Band playing opposite University one day. I was indifferent, and for the time ignorant and incapable of knowing, whether the music was that of Wagner or Sousa. It seemed to me the music of Apollo, certainly of some one grander than all grand composers. And yet, as I was informed, what I had entirely loved was from an inferior opera which every street boy can improve.

It was another music, and yet symphonious, that I heard, when I came again to Addison's Walk at Magdalen. I stopped at Magdalen cloisters on my way—

Oxford

O blessed shades ! O gentle cool retreat
From all th' immoderate Heat
In which the frantic World does burn and sweat !—

Let any one who has laughed at Oxford discipline, or criticised her system of education, go there in the morning early and be abased before the solemnity of that square lawn ; and should he be left with a desire to explain anything, let him take up his abode with the stony mysterious beasts gathered around that lawn. I like that grass amidst the cloisters because it is truly common. No one, I hope and believe, except a gardener, an emblem, is permitted to walk thereon. It belongs to me and to you and to the angels. Such an emerald in such a setting is a fit symbol of the university, and its privy seal.

It is still unnecessary to pass an examination before entering Addison's walk. It is therefore unfrequented. A financier made a pretty sum one Midsummer-day by accepting gratuities from all the strangers who came to its furthest point—"a custom older than King Alfred." But, although they are not vulgarly so called, these walks are the final school of the Platonist. It is an elucidation of the Phædo to pace therein. That periwinkle-bordered pathway is the place of long thoughts that come home with circling footsteps again and again. It is the home of beech and elm, and of whatsoever that is beautiful and wise and stately dwells among beech and elm.

More than one college history is linked with a tree. Lincoln College reverently entreats the solitary plane

8

tree. William of Waynfleet commanded that Magdalen College should be built over against the oak that fell after six hundred years of life a century ago. Sir Thomas White was " warned in a dream " to build a college at a place where there stood a triple elm tree. Hence arose St. John's College. Two hundred years ago the tree was known to exist, and there is ground for the pious belief that a scion still flourishes there.

Nowhere is green so wonderful as at Magdalen or Trinity. But their sweetness is no more than the highest expression of the privacy of Oxford. Turn aside at the gate that lies nearest your path ; enter ; and you will find a cloister or cloistral calm, free from wolf and ass. " The walks at these times," said a vacation visitor, " are so much one's own—the tall trees of Christ's, the groves of Magdalen ! The halls deserted, and with open doors inviting one to slip in unperceived, and pay a devoir to some Founder, or noble or royal Benefactress (that should have been ours) whose portrait seems to smile upon their overlooked beadsman and to adopt me for their own. Then, to take a peep in by the way at the butteries, and sculleries, redolent of antique hospitality ; the immense caves of kitchens, kitchen fire-places, cordial recesses ; ovens where the first pies were baked four centuries ago ; and spits which have cooked for Chaucer ! Not the meanest minister among the dishes but is hallowed to me through his imagination, and the Cook goes forth a Manciple." With a little effrontery and an English accent you may enjoy the inmost bowers of the Fellows

Oxford

or, *Si qua est ea gloria*, gather fruit from the espaliers of the president. The walls are barricaded only with ivy, or wallflower, or the ivy-leaved toadflax and its delicate bells. But the stranger never learns that the seclusion of Oxford is perennial, and that only in the vacations may he suffer from what the old pun calls *porta eburna*. The place is habitually almost deserted, except by the ghosts of the dead. Returning to it, when friends are gone, and every one is a stranger, the echoes of our footsteps in the walls are as the voices of our dead selves ; we are among the ghosts ; the past is omnipotent, even terrible. Echoes, quotes Montaigne, are the spirits of the dead, and among these mouldering stones we may put our own interpretation upon that. And no one that has so returned, or that comes a reverent stranger for the first time to Oxford, can read without deep intelligence the lines which are put into the mouth of Lacordaire in " Ionica " :—

> Lost to the Church and deaf to me, this town
> Yet wears the reverend garniture of peace.
> Set in a land of trade, like Gideon's fleece
> Bedewed where all is dry ; the Pope may frown ;
> But, if this city is the shrine of youth,
> How shall the Preacher lord of virgin souls,
> When by glad streams and laughing lawns he strolls,
> How can he bless them not ? Yet in sad sooth,
> When I would love those English gownsmen, sighs
> Heave my frail breast, and weakness dims mine eyes.
> These strangers heed me not—far off in France
> Are young men not so fair, and not so cold,
> My listeners. Were they here, their greeting glance
> Might charm me to forget that I were old.

Some time ago I went into a grey quadrangle, filled

On Entering Oxford

with gusty light and the crimson of creeper-leaves, tremulous or already in flight. A tall poplar, the favourite of the months from April to October, was pensively distributing its foliage upon the grass. There, the leaves became invisible, because of brilliant frost, and in a high attic I heard once again the laud or summons or complaint of bells. That was All Saints'; that, St. Mary's ; that, the Cathedral's ; and that was their blended after-tone, seeming to come from the sky. Each bell had its own character or mood, sometimes constant, sometimes changing with the weather of the night. One, for example, spoke out sullenly and ceased, as if to return to musing that had been painfully interrupted. Another bell seemed to take deep joy in its frequent melodious duty—like some girl seated alone in her bower at easy toil, now and then lifting her head, and with her embroidery upon her knee, chanting joys past and present and yet to come. Once again I felt the mysterious pleasure of being in an elevated Oxford chamber at night, among cloud and star,—so that I seemed to join in the inevitable motion of the planets,—and as I saw the sea of roofs and horned turrets and spires I knew that, although architecture is a dead language, here at least it speaks strongly and clearly, pompous as Latin, subtle as Greek. I used to envy the bell-ringers on days of ancient festival or recent victory, and cannot wonder that old Anthony à Wood should have noted the eight bells of Merton as he came home from antiquarian walks, and would often ring those same bells " for recreation's

On Entering Oxford

Duke Humphrey's library was the nest from which Bodley's august collection overflowed ; the very timber of the Bodleian was in part Merton's gift. No city preserves the memory and signature of so many men. The past and the dead have here, as it were, a corporate life. They are an influence, an authority ; they create and legislate to-day. Everything in the present might have been foretold, and in fact existed in some latent form, in the past, as Merlin was said to have foretold the migration of Oxford scholars from Cricklade, *i.e.* Greeklade. Therefore, in Oxford alone, as I walk, I seem to be in the living past. The oldest thing is not as in most places a curiosity. Since it is told of Oxford, the story is not lightly to be discredited, that Ludovicus Vives, who was sent as professor of rhetoric by Wolsey, was welcomed by a swarm of bees, and that they, " to signify the incomparable sweetness of his eloquence," settled under the leads of his study at Corpus Christi College, and there for a hundred and thirty years continued, until they dispersed out of sorrow for the fallen Stuart family. When dawn arrives to the student, after a night among books, and the towers and spires seem to be just fresh from the acting of some stately drama ; or at nightfall, when the bells ring as he comes, joyful and tired, home from the west,—then the city and all its component ages speak out, as if the past were but a fine memory, richly stored and ordered.

Once, answering the call of one of those bells that are to a scholar as a trumpet to a soldier, I found myself at a service that had in it elements older than Oxford. I was surely at a Greek festival. The genial, flushed, slightly grotesque faces of the College fellows contrasted with the white children of the choir, very much as the swarthy faun with the young god in Titian's " Bacchus and Ariadne." The notes of the choristers and of the organ were moulded to finer results by the severe decorations of the carven stone around and above. When one sang alone, it was as it had been a dove floating to the windows and away, away. There were parts of the music so faint and so exquisitely blended that the twenty voices were but as the sound of a reverberating bell. A voice of baser metal read the lesson with a melancholy dignity that made the words at once pleasing and unintelligible. When the last surplice had floated past the exit, the worshippers looked a little pained and confused, as if doubting whether they had not assisted some beautiful rash heresy. Turning into High Street, I was rudely called back from a fantastic visit to Tempe, by the wind and rain of every day. The usual pageant of study and pleasure was passing up and down.

Here was a smiling gentleman, red as the opening morn, with black clothes, white tie,—one who scoffs at everything but gout. He notes in the fragrance of his favourite dishes omens of greater import than augurs used to read from sacrificial victims.

Here was a pale seraph, his eyes commercing with the sky. He has taken every possible prize. Nobody but his friends can think that he is uninteresting.

On Entering Oxford

Here was a little, plain-featured, gentle ascetic, one of the "last enchantments of the middle ages" that are to be seen still walking about Oxford. Five hundred years ago he might have ridden, "coy as a maid," to Canterbury and told "the clerk of Oxford's tale." Now, the noises of the world are too much for him, and he murmurs among his trees—

> How safe, methinks, and strong behind
> These trees have I encamped my mind,
> Where beauty aiming at the heart,
> Bends in some tree its useless dart,
> And where the world no certain shot
> Can make, or me it toucheth not,
> But I on it securely play,
> And gall its horsemen all the day.
> Bind me, ye woodbines in your twines.
> Curl me about, ye gadding vines,
> And oh so close your circles lace,
> That I may never leave this place !

Here was a youth not much past seventeen. In his face the *welt schmerz* contends with the pride in his last *bon mot*. He is a wide and subtle reader ; he has contributed to the halfpenny press. He has materialised spirits and moved objects at a distance. In the world, there is little left for him except repose and weak tea.

Here was one that might be a monk and might equally well be St. Michael, with flashing eyes and high white forehead that catches a light from beyond the dawn and glows. He is a splendour among men as he walks in the crowd of high churchmen, low churchmen, broad churchmen, nonconformists, and men who on Sunday wear bowler hats.

Oxford

Here was a shy don, married to Calliope—a brilliant companion—one who shares a wisdom as deep and almost as witty as Montaigne's, with a few fellows of colleges, and ever murmuring " Codex."

Here was one, watched over alike by the Muses and the Graces ; honey-tongued ; athletic ; who would rather spend a life in deciding between the Greek and Roman ideals than in ruling Parliament and being ruled by society.   He strode like a Plantagenet.   When he stood still he was a classical Hermes.

Here was a Blue " with shy but conscious look " ; and there the best of all Vices.

Here was a youth, with gaudy tie, who believed that he was leading a bull-dog, but showed a wise acquiescence in the intricate canine etiquette.   May his dog not cease before him.

Here was a martial creature, walking six miles an hour, pensively, in his master's gown.   His beard, always blown over his shoulder, has been an inspiration to generations of undergraduates, and, with his bellying gown, gives him a resemblance to Boreas or Notus.

Probably because the able novelist has not visited Oxford, men move about its streets more naïvely and with more expression in their faces than anywhere else in the world.   There you may do anything but carry a walking-stick.   (As I write, fashion has changed her mind, and walking-sticks of the more flippant kinds are commonly in use.)   There are therefore more unmasked faces in half of Turl Street than in the whole of the Strand.   Almost every one appears to have

16

On Entering Oxford

a sense of part proprietorship in the city; walks as if he were in his own garden; has no fear lest he should be caught smiling to himself, or, as midnight approaches, even singing loudly to himself. A don will not hesitate to make the worst joke in a strong and cheerful voice in the bookseller's shop, when it is full of clever freshmen.

Yonder they go, the worldly and the unworldly, the rich and poor, high and low, proving that Oxford is one of the most democratic places in Europe. The lax discipline that broadens the horizon of the inexpert stranger is probably neither unwise nor unpremeditated. It is certainly not inconsistent with the genius of a city whose very stones may be supposed to have acquired an educative faculty, and a sweet presence that is not to be put by. No fool ever went up without becoming at least a coxcomb before he came down. In no place are more influences brought to bear upon the mind, though it is emphatically a place where a man is expected to educate himself. A man is apt to feel on first entering Oxford, and still more on leaving it, that the beautiful city is unfortunate in having but mortal minds to teach. There is a keen and sometimes pathetic sense of a great music which one cannot wholly follow, a light unapprehended, a wisdom not realised. Yet much is to be guessed at or privily understood, when we behold St. Mary's spire, marvellously attended, and crowned, when the night is one sapphire, by Cassiopeia. And the ghosts take shape—the cowled, mitred, mail-coated, sceptred company of founders, benefactors, master-masons, scholars, philosophers, and the later soldiers, poets, statesmen, and wits, and finally some one, among the rich in influence of yesterday, who embodies for one or another of us the sweetness of the place.

For me, when the first splendour of the city in my imagination has somewhat grown dim, I see in the midst and on high, a room, little wider than the thickness of its walls, which were part stone, part books; for the books fitted naturally into the room, leaving spaces only for a bust of Plato, a portrait of Sir Thomas Browne, a decanter, and a window commanding sky and clouds and stars above an horizon of many towers. There, too, is a great fire; a dowager brown teapot; with a pair of slippers,—and to get into them was no whit less magical than into the seven-league boots. I see a chair also, where a man might sit, curled, with the largest folio and be hidden. I guess at the face of the man under the folio. He was a small, shrunken, elvish figure, with a smile like the first of June often budding in a face like the last of December. In rest, that face was grim as if carved in limestone; in expression, like waters in Spring. His curled, ebony hair had a singular freshness and hint of vitality that gave the lie to his frail form and husky voice. Cut in wood, the large nose and chin, peering forward, would have served well as the figure-head of a merry ship, and to me he seemed indeed to travel on such a ship towards a land that no other man desires. His talk was ever of men, fighting, ploughing, singing; and how fair women be;

On Entering Oxford

with jests and fancies that disenthroned all powers except fantasy and adventure and mirth. Out of doors, at Yarnton or Cumnor or Tew, he seemed near kinsman to the sun and the south wind, so that for a time we were one with them, with a sense of mystery and of pride. And, whether in or out of doors, he loved the night, because her hands were soft, and he found the shadows *infernis hilares sine regibus*, as in the world of Saturn. He would hail the morn as he saw her from a staircase window with " Sweet cousin " and such follies ; and would go into the chapel on summer evenings without a candle to see prophet and apostle lit by the tender beam. He wrote, and never printed, much verse. When I look at it now, I wonder in what language it was conceived, and where the key is hidden, and by what shores and forests to-day, men speak or dream it. The verses seem to maturer eyes but as crude translations out of silence. Yet in the old days we called him sometimes the Last, sometimes the First, of the Bards, so nimble and radiant was his spirit. He seemed one that might have written *Tamerlane* in his youth, after a pot of sack with Shakespeare at the " Crown " in Cornmarket Street. I know not whether to call him immemorially old or young. He had touches of the golden age, and as it were a tradition from the singer who was in that ship which

First through the Euxine seas bore all the flower of Greece.

Unlike other clever people in Oxford he was brilliant in early morning ; would rise and talk and write at dawn,—go a-maying,—sing hunting ditties amid the snow to the leaden east and the frozen starlings, by Marston or above Wytham and Eynsham. His laugh fell upon our ears like an echo from long-forgotten, Arcadian existences ; it was in harmony with the songs of thrushes and the murmur of the Evenlode. Coming into his room we expected to see a harp at his side. But where are the voices that we heard and uttered ?—

> Are they exiled out of stony breasts,
> Never to make return ?

Once more is the blackbird's fluting a mystery save that it speaks of him, last of the Bards.

"Beautiful Mother," he sang, to Oxford, "too old not to be sad, too austere to look sad and to mourn! Sometimes thou art young to my eyes because thy children are always young, and for a little while it was a journey to youth itself to visit thee. More often, not only art thou old and austere, but thy fresh and youthful children seem to have learned austerity and the ways of age, for love of thee, graciously apparelling their youth,—so that I have met old Lyly in Holywell, and Johnson at the Little Clarendon Street bookshop, and Newman by Iffley rose-window,—with their age taken away, by virtue of a mellower light upon thy lawns and a mellower shade under thy towers, than other cities. Or have I truly heard thee weep when the last revelry is quiet, and the scholar by his lamp sees thee as thou wast and wilt be, and the moonlight has her will with the spires and gardens?

On Entering Oxford

Oh, to the sad how pleasant thy age, to the joyous how admirable thy youth! Yet to the wise, perhaps, thou art neither young nor old, but eternal ; and not so much beautiful as Beauty herself, masked as Cybele! And perhaps, oh sweet and wise and solemn mother, thou wilt not hear unkindly thy latest froward courtier, or at least will let him pass unnoticed, since one that speaks of thee,

"Cannot dispraise without a kind of praise.

Or will it more delight thee to be praised in a tongue that is out of time, as thou seemest out of space and time ?—

"Vive Midae gazis et Lydo ditior auro
Troica et Euphratea super diademata felix,
Quem non ambigui fasces, non mobile vulgus,
Non leges, non castra tenent, qui pectore magno
Spemque metumque domas. Nos, vilia turba, caducis
Deservire bonis semperque optare parati,
Spargimur in casus. Celsa tu mentis ab arce
Despicis errantes, humanaque gaudia rides."

THE STONES OF OXFORD

Oxford

held the University chest in the beginning, representative of Oxford's piety and generosity. On the east, in the High Street, University College and St. Mary's and Brasenose speak clearly, although falsely, of King Alfred. There, by St. Peter's in the East, was the old east gate ; and in sight of these is Merton, the fount of the collegiate idea. On the north, in Cornmarket Street, St. Michael's marks the place of the north gate, and while it is one of the oldest, is by far the oldest-looking place in Oxford, rising up always to our surprise, like a piece of substantial night left by the dark ages, yet clothed with green in June. On the west, the Castle tower, twin made with St. Michael's by the first Norman lord of Oxford, lies by the old west gate ; and the quiet, monstrous mound beyond recalls the days of King Alfred's daughter's supremacy in Mercia. At Carfax itself there was a St. Martin's church, of which only the tower remains, a descendant of the one whose bells in the Middle Ages and again in the seventeenth century, called the city to arms against the University, but long ago deprived of its insolent height of tower, because the citizens pelted the scholars therefrom.

Moved by the presence of a city whose strange beauty was partly interpreted from these vigorous hieroglyphics, mediæval and later men, who had the advantage of living before history was invented, framed for it a divine or immensely ancient origin. Even kings, or such as quite certainly existed, were deemed unworthy to be the founders. We believe now that the first mention of Oxford was as an inconsiderable but progressive township in the reign of Edward the Elder, Alfred's son : but those old lovers attributed to Alfred the restoration of a university that was in his time old and honoured ; and some said that he endowed three doctors of grammar, arts, and theology, there ; others, less precise than those who put the foundation of Cambridge at 4317 B.C., discovered that Oxford was founded by the Trojans who (as used to be well known) came to Britain from their burning city. But to Oxford the Trojans brought certain Greek philosophers, and at that early date illustrated the universal hospitality and independence of nationality and language that were so characteristic, before the place became a Stuart park. And as the Athenians had in their city and its attendant landscape all those natural beauties and utilities which make possible a peerless academy, so also had the Britons, says Anthony à Wood, herein agreeing with Polydore Vergil, " when by a remnant of the Grecians, that came amongst them, they or their successors selected such a place in Britain to plant a school or schools therein, which for its pleasant situation was afterwards called *Bellositum* or *Bellosite*, now Oxford." Among these generous suppositions or dreams was the story that Apollo, at the downfall of the Olympians, flying now to Rome and now to Athens, found at last something congenial in the brown oak woods and silver waters of Oxford, and a bride in the puissant nymph of Isis ; on which favoured site, as was fitting, there afterwards arose a place, with the learning and architectural beauty of Athens, the divine

27

Oxford

inspiration of Delphi, and the natural loveliness of Delos . . .

There is, said Anthony à Wood, "an old tradition that goeth from father to son of our inhabitants, which much derogateth from the antiquity of this city—and that is : When Frideswyde had bin soe long absent from hence, she came from Binsey (triumphing with her virginity) into the city mounted on a milk-white ox betokening innocency ; and as she rode along the streets, she would forsooth be still speaking to her ox, ' Ox forth,' ' Ox forth ' or (as 'tis related) ' *bos perge* ' (that is, ' ox goe on,' or ' ox (goe on) forth ')—and hence they indiscreetly say that our city was from thence called Oxforth or Oxford."

But there has never been composed a quite appropriately magnificent legend that could be received by the faithful as the canonical fiction for Oxford, as the *Aeneid* is for Rome ; and now there can never be.

There is, however, still a pleasant haze (that might encourage a poet or a herald) suspended over the early history of Oxford. It is unlikely that the place was of importance in Roman times ; later, its position on a river and a boundary brought it many sufferings at the hands of Dane and Saxon. But no one need fear to believe that, early in the eighth century, Didan, an under king, and his daughter Frideswide established there a nunnery and built a church of stone, now perhaps mingled with the later masonry. It was rebuilt by Ethelred in the eleventh century with a quite exceptional fineness in the Saxon workmanship ; and was girdled by the churches of St. Martin, St. George, St. Mary Magdalen, St. Mary the Virgin, St. Ebbe, St. Michael, and St. Peter in the East ; and the last two, to one who had stood at Carfax in 1100, would still be recognised, if he visited the shadowed doorway and stern crypt of the one, and the tower of the other, though he might look in vain for what he knew in " The Seven Deadly Sins lane " and elsewhere.

Whatever learning then flourished in the city is now to be found in its architecture, in Prior Philip's book on the miracles of St. Frideswide, and in the inestimable atmosphere of the place. We can guess that there was much that is worthy to be known, from the eloquent monkish figures of the corbels in Christ Church chapter-house ; and can wistfully think of the wisdom that was uttered in Beaumont, the royal palace and learned resort, whose gardens lay at Broken Hays and near Worcester College ; and in Osney Abbey, whose bells —Hautclere, Douce, Clement, Austin, Marie, Gabriel et John—made music that was known to the Eynsham abbot on May evenings, when it was a rich, calm retreat, and not as now, a shadowy outline and a sorrowful heap of stones beyond the railway station. More than the ghost of the abbey survives in the sketch of its ruined but still noble walls, in the background of that picture of its last abbot, in a window of the south choir aisle at Christ Church.

Before the Conquest Oxford had been visited by parliaments and kings ; it now began to be honoured by learning and art. *Olim truncus eram . . . .*

maluit esse deum. It had often been violated or burned ; in Doomsday Book it appears as a half desolate city, despite the churches; but it had already begun, though again checked by fire that flew among the wooden houses with such ghastly ease, to assume the proportions and the grace which were fostered by William of Wykeham and a hundred of the great unknown, and in the last few years by Aldrich and Wren and Jones,—crowned by the munificence of Radcliffe, —illuminated with green and white and gold and purple by the unremembered and by Reynolds, Morris, and Burne-Jones. The Saxon work at St. Frideswide's was superseded or veiled by the Norman architects ; the fine old pillars were in part altered or replaced; and the relics of the Saint herself were transferred ceremoniously and " with all the sweet odours and spices imaginable," to a more imposing place of rest. Upon the base of the old fortifications probably now rose the bastions of the mediæval city wall, once so formidable but now defensive only against time, and unable any longer to make history, but only poetry, as they stand peacefully and muffled with herbage in New College Gardens, or at Merton or Pembroke, or by the churchyard of St. Peter's in the East.

The history of that age in Oxford is indistinct, and recorded events therein have a suddenness, for modern readers, which is vivid and fascinating, but to the historian at least, painful and false. And so the birth of the University, in the midst of darkness and noise, is to us to-day a melodious sudden cry. It is as if a voice, unexpectedly arose, calling—and the words are said to have been used by two poor Irish students in an ignorant and worldly land—"Here is wisdom for sale! Come, buy!" We know that famous lecturers from the continental universities came; but not with what eloquence and applause they spoke. It may confidently be surmised that there was something sweet to learned minds in the air or tradition of the place. The walls are fallen or forgotten that heard the prelusive lectures of Pullein and Vacarius; and the brilliant Franciscan house in St. Benedict's is chiefly known by its influence in the founding of Balliol, and by the greatest school-men, its alumni. But if we go to the grey domestic little lodgings, with "arms and rebusses that are depicted and cut in stone over each door," vestiges of a Benedictine scholastic house, at Worcester College, we may fancifully pierce beyond John Giffard's foundation and the preceding Carmelites, to the earliest lovers of learning who loved Oxford too. At St. Mary's the work of the fancy is easier and more sure. There the University books, and there a money chest, reposed. There were the highest deliberations and ceremonies. There a man was graduated, and from its porch he passed out a clerk of Oxford.

If the University was early associated with a place of holiness and beauty, still more firmly was it rooted in a becoming poverty. It had neither a roof nor a certain purse. For years it had not a name. The University was in fact but a spirit of wisdom and grace; men had heard of it and sought it; and where one or two were gathered together to take advantage of it, there was her school and her only endowment. Now and then to such a group came in a legacy of books or gold. But that was a crop for which no one sowed, and before it was possible, it had been rumoured that there was something in Oxford not visible, yet very present and necessary; and scholars came with as great zeal as was ever cherished by reports of gold. They brought what in their devotion they came to seek. Thus Gerald of Wales came, and for three days read aloud his glorious book to large audiences. Every day was marked by sumptuous and generous feasts. It was, indeed, "a costly and noble act," as he says himself, "for the authentic and ancient times of the poets were thus in some measure renewed." Carmelites, Dominicans, and Franciscans, and vivid men from the University of Paris, came to teach. Even then, the University quarrelled with the town over the price of victuals and rooms, and invaded the extortionate Jew. There, about the streets, walked the magnificent Franciscans, Roger Bacon and Grosseteste, and the pure and gracious and learned St. Thomas Cantelupe.

Early in the thirteenth century there was a Chancellor set over the scholars by the Bishop of Lincoln, in whose diocese Oxford lay. Very soon the Chancellor was elected by the University; and the Masters in congregation could legislate, and sometimes did, although questions were often effectually decided by a popular vote among the students,—who also themselves chose by vote the heads of their hostels or halls. For there were, at an early date, houses already associated with learning, and governed either by a common landlord or by a scholar of some standing and age. There a man might read, and comfort himself according to his means, and finally at night stamp up and down a passage, to warm his feet, before going to sleep in a crowded bed-chamber. On any day there was a chance that some splendid man, coming a little in the rear of his fame, would arrive in Oxford, and lecture or read a book. Should kings, or priests, or rude citizens interfere, the scholar could rusticate voluntarily—as he sometimes did—at Stamford, or Reading, or Maidstone, or Cambridge, and there, as best he might, by study and self-denial, as by a sacrament, recreate the University. The City, and until our own time the Crown, had to pay in round sums for such an insult as the hanging of several scholars ; the money lined the bottom of St. Frideswide's chest. A man with no possessions but the leaf of a manuscript, or a dagger, or a cloak, left it with the keepers of the chest as security for a loan, whether he were Welsh, or Hungarian, or Italian, or French.

An Englishman, William of Durham, who had enjoyed the University hospitality at Paris, first kindled the flame which was to be kept burning by so many afterwards, as a *focus perennis* for the homeless student. He left Paris after a town-and-gown quarrel, along with many French students, whom Henry III. welcomed to Oxford in 1229. William went to Rome, before returning to England, and remembered Oxford when he lay dying at Rouen—perchance reminded there of the city which until fifty years ago was equal with it in ancient beauty, and has been clouded in the same way. He left in his will a sum of money to the University. It was employed in making more steadfast abodes for Oxford students; at a house, for example, that stood on the site of the bookseller's shop opposite University College lodge. This act is counted the foundation of University College, with its original four masters, who shall be thought "most fit to advance or profit in the Holy Church and who have not to live handsomely without it in the state of Masters of Arts."

There had previously been similar Halls, and many were afterwards founded,—Hawk Hall, Perilous Hall, Elm Hall, Winton Hall, Beef Hall, Greek Hall, Segrim Hall; in fact so large a number that half the Oxford inns are or were perversions of the old Halls; and even tradesmen who are not innkeepers now make their rich accounts among the ghosts of forgotten principals. These had not in them the necessary statutes and "great bases for eternity" which a college deserves. But henceforward there were some fortunate students who might indeed have to sing or make Latin verses in order to earn a bed, or a crust and a pot of ale, while making their way to or from Oxford; but, once there, they were sure of such a home as no other place, unless, perhaps, the place of their nativity, could give.

"It is all," says Newman, speaking of a college, "and does all that is implied in the name of home. Youths, who have left the maternal roof, and travelled some hundred miles for the acquisition of knowledge, find an

The Stones of Oxford

altera Troja and *simulata Pergama* at the end of their journey and their place of temporary sojourn. Home is for the youth, who knows nothing of the world, and who would be forlorn and sad, if thrown upon it. It is the refuge of helpless boyhood, which would be famished and pine away if it were not maintained by others. It is the providential shelter of the weak and inexperienced who have still to learn how to cope with the temptations which lie outside of it. It is the place of training for those who are not only ignorant, but have not yet learned how to learn, and who have to be taught, by careful individual trial, how to set about profiting by the lessons of a teacher. And it is the school of elementary studies, not of advanced ; for such studies alone can boys at best apprehend and master. Moreover, it is the shrine of our best affections, the bosom of our fondest recollections, a spell upon our after life, a stay for world-weary mind and soul, wherever we are cast, till the end comes. Such are the attributes or offices of home, and like to these in one or other sense and measure, are the attributes and offices of a College in a University."

In the unconscious preparation for such a place William of Durham was the first to leave money ; the founders of Balliol the first to gather a number of scholars under one roof, with a corporate life, and as we may assume, a set of customary, unwritten laws ; but Walter de Merton was the first to endow and provide with tenements and statutes a college, in all important respects, like a college of to-day,—a place even at that time standing in a genial avuncular relationship towards

35

The Stones of Oxford

the spire of the church of St. Mary the Virgin first rose against the sky. Then also the ashes of St. Frideswide were promoted to a new and more precious place of rest. The sculptor at work upon the shrine had evidently at his side the leaves of maple and crowfoot and columbine, ivy and sycamore and oak, hawthorn and bryony, from the neighbouring woods, where the saint had lain in hiding or ministered to the calamities of the poor ; and perhaps the season was late autumn, for among the oak leaves are acorns, and some of the cups are empty. All these things he carved on the base of the shrine.

It was of this period that the story was told that two barefooted, hungry travellers from the west were approaching Oxford, and had come in sight of it near Cumnor, when they found a beautiful woman seated by the wayside. So beautiful was she that they knelt at her feet, "being simple men." *Salve Regina!* they cried. Then, she bending forward and speaking, they were first surprised that she should speak to them ; and next ventured to speak to her, and ask her name. Whereat she "raised her small golden head so that in the sun her hair seemed to flow and flow continually down," and looked towards Oxford. There two spires and two towers could just be seen betwixt the oak trees. "My name," she said, "is known to all men save you. It is Pulchritudo. And that," as she pointed to the shining stones of the city, "is my home." Those two were silent, between amazement and joy, until one said "It is our Lady!" and the other "Lo! it is Venus, and she sits upon many waters yonder." Hardly had they resumed their ordinary pace when they found an old man, seated by the wayside, very white and yet "very pleasant and alluring to behold." So to him also the simple wayfarers knelt down. Then that old man bent forward and spoke to them with golden words, and only the one who had called the beautiful woman "Venus" dared to speak. He it was that questioned the old man about the woman and about himself. "My name is Sapientia," he said, and "that is my home," he continued, and looked towards Oxford, where two spires and two towers could just be seen betwixt the oak trees. "And," he concluded solemnly, "that woman is my mother and she grows not old." The men went their way, one saying, "It is a place of lies"; the other saying, "It is wonderful"; and when they looked back the old man and the beautiful woman had vanished. In the city they were often seen, but the two strangers could not speak with them, "for they were greatest in the city of Oxford. Some said that he was an Austin friar and she a light woman; but they are not to be believed." And when they had dwelt in Oxford a short time and had seen "what store of pious and learned and illuminated books were in the Halls, and what costly and fine things in its churches and Convents," the one said, "I believe that what Sapientia and Pulchritudo said was the truth"; and the other said, "Truly, the city is worthy of them both"; wherefore they dwelt there until their deaths, and found it "the most loving and lovely city" in Christendom.

The Stones of Oxford

Dervorguilla and Walter de Merton had thus made the University a father and a mother to the scholar. For a time, indeed, the principals had often to transfer their *penates* ; the founder's inheritors lived in scattered tenements which they changed from necessity or choice, now and then ; yet they had the imperishable sentiment of home, and for some years they had little more, except in a small degree at Merton and Queen's, since the colleges neither demanded nor provided that the scholars should study according to rule.

Under Edward II. Exeter College was founded, and linked from the beginning with the west country, by the simultaneous co-foundation of a school, and the rule that all the scholars should thence be drawn. Decent poverty and love of learning were the other qualifications of a scholar. Then followed Oriel, with Edward II. as its founder, the advowson of the Church of St. Mary the Virgin as part of its support, and its name derived from the Hall of La Oriole, which it received early, and soon afterwards occupied. Its library was the first college library ; but the acquirement was technically defective, and the Fellows of Oriel could not resist the students who broke in and carried away the books. Fellows and admirers repaired the loss.

Philippa, Queen of Edward III., was joined with her chaplain in the foundation of Queen's College " for the cultivation of Theology, to the glory of God, the advance of the Church, and the salvation of souls." A little subtlety on the part of the founder and sentiment on the part of the queens, enabled the college to exchange compliments with Anne of Bohemia, Henrietta Maria, Charlotte and Adelaide. The founder was a Cumberland man, and his college attracted a neighbour or a man who spoke with his accent or had the same traditions to become one of the fellows, equal in number with Christ and His apostles. Before and after the beginning of colleges, men from the same district made a small "new Scotland" or "new France" in Oxford streets. Thus the scholars of St. George's and Oriel were for some time largely Welsh; at Balliol and University College there were many northerners. At all times these divisions were emphasised by conflicts with tongue and arrow and sword. Scholars overlooked their Aristotle at bloody arguments in Grove Street and Cornmarket, between North and South, Irish and Welsh and Scotch, in combinations that varied unaccountably or according to the politics of the day. You might know a scholar, as an ancient tinker remarked the other day, remembering the boxing booths of his youth, by the way he fought. The election of a chancellor, or a church wake, and an exchange of lusty oaths between men of two parties were the occasion. In later years Realists and Nominalists,—Orthodox and Wycliffites, —now and then reduced their disagreement to simple terms. Nor were the citizens with difficulty persuaded to take or make a side in the disputes, whether they encountered the scholars at inns, or as they stood on market-days,—the sellers of hay and faggots and hogs, stretching in their regular places from the East gate, in front of St. Mary's and All Saints', to Carfax and the

The Stones of Oxford

Cross Inn. Once, a northern chaplain, "with other malefactors," embattled themselves and sought out the Welshmen with bent bows, crying to the " Welsh dogs and their whelps " that an Owen or a Meredydd who looked out at his door was a dead man. The Welshmen were driven out of the city with ignominy and blood. The Northeners robbed and murdered indiscriminately, and destroyed not only books but harps, until, finding an ale-house, they were incontinently appeased. On another occasion some townsmen burst in, on a Sunday, upon a few scholars, wounding and despoiling them. The scholars spread their story and collected friends. The townsmen responded to the sound of horns and St. Martin's bell. Countrymen from Hinksey and Headington came to the help of the unlearned. The air whistled and hummed with the flight of arrows and stones ; the streets were crimsoned. But the reverend gentleman who led the learned was untimely shot down, and his cause evaporated. Some scholars fled to the country, some to sanctuary, and were comforted by the excommunication and fining of their opponents. After a similar fight the University was allowed that exemption from the city courts which it still enjoys. In fact, the disturbances earned very cheaply for the University concessions which put the citizens at a disadvantage, and emphasised distinctions, so as to cause other disturbances in turn. Henry V., himself a Queen's College man, at last interfered with an order that scholars would only be treated as such if they were under the rule of an approved head. It was an attempt to banish the wild errant scholars, often Irish-men, and to make a common type of Chaucer's Clerk of Oxenford, who had been to Padua and knew Petrarch's verse. He was one who, even in his devotion to books, did not forget the souls of his benefactors, for which he was, in the first instance, endowed to pray—

> And he was not right fat, I undertake,
> But looked holwe, and therto sobrely ;
> Ful thredbare was his overeste courtepy ;
> For he hadde geten hym yet no benefice,
> Ne was so worldly for to have office ;
> For hym was levere have at his beddes heed
> Twenty bookes clad in black or reed
> Of Aristotle and his philosophie,
> Than robës riche, or fithele, or gay sautrie ;
> But al be that he was a philosophre,
> Yet hadde he but litel gold in cofre ;
> But al that he myghte of his freendes hente
> On bookes and his lernynge he it spent,
> And bisily gan for the soules preye
> Of him that yaf hym wherewith to scoleye.
> Of studie tooke he moost cure and moost heede,
> Noght o word spake he moore than was neede,
> And that was seyd in forme and reverence,
> And short and quyk and ful of hy sentence.
> Sounynge in moral vertu was his speche,
> And gladly wolde he lerne and gladly teche.

But William of Wykeham, before that time, had given to New College a code of ornate and intricate rules for morals and manners, which became a legacy to the University at large ; and in the first place checked the savage liberties of scholars ; in the second, helped to make learning more " humane," to make the " Arts " the " humanities." He built a chapel for the exclusive use of the scholars of his foundation. That in itself was an inestimable addition to the golden chain by which Oxford holds the memories of men. To the chapel they were to go every day, and there to say their *Paters* and *Aves*. Its Latin—the fittest language to be uttered amidst old architecture—and its coloured windows alone are not to-day as they were in Wykeham's time. He built the bell-tower and the cloisters, and so gave to generations a pleasant vision, and—when dreams are on the wing—a starting-place or an eyrie for dreams. He built also a kitchen, a brewery, and a bakehouse. He stocked both a garden and a library for college use. Long before the " first tutor of the first college of the first University of the world " entered Oxford with post horses to assert his position, the Warden of New College had the use of six horses. He wore an ermine amice in chapel. He had his own palace apart. But the humblest member of the foundation had been as minutely provided for by Wykeham's code. Above all, the scholar was not to be left to himself in his studies, but to the care of an appointed tutor. And in 1387 the new college proceeded to William of Wykeham's quadrangle, with singing and pomp. It was the first home of scholars in Oxford, which was completely and specially fashioned for their use alone, to be

> A place of friends ! a place of books !
> A place of good things olden !

In the next century the ideas of Walter de Merton and Dervorguilla and William of Wykeham were borrowed and developed by loving founders, architects, and benefactors. The building of Lincoln College, next founded, was begun as soon as its charter was received ; a chapel and a library, a hall and a kitchen, and chambers on three storys, finely and nobly built, were a matter of course. In the same way, All Souls' front quadrangle, practically as we see it to-day, was built at once by Archbishop Chichele, the founder ; and at Magdalen, which was next founded, the tower began to rise on the extreme east of the city, to salute the rising sun with its pinnacles, and on May morning, with a song of choristers.

For Oxford, the fifteenth century was an age of libraries and books. Looking back upon it, Duke Humphrey of Gloucester seems its patron saint,— donor of books to the Benedictines who lived on the site of Worcester College, and to the University,— harbinger of the Bodleian. We can still catch the savour of the old libraries at Merton where the light coloured by painted glass used to inlay the gloom under the wooden roof, or behind the quiet latticed windows above the cloisters at Christ Church. "What pleasantness of teaching there is in books, how easy, how secret," says Richard de Bury, Bishop of Durham, an old Oxford man, and the giver of the first library to Oxford. "They are masters who instruct us without rod or ferule, without angry words, without clothes or money. If you come to them, they are not asleep; if you ask and inquire of them, they do not withdraw themselves ; they do not chide if you make mistakes ; they do not laugh at you if you are ignorant. O books, who alone are liberal and free, who give to all who ask of you and enfranchise all who serve you faithfully! by how many types ye are commended to learned men in the Scriptures given us by the inspiration of God! . . . Ye are the wells of living waters, which father Abraham first digged, Isaac digged again, and which the Philistines strive to fill up! . . ." Bury was a friend of Petrarch and Bradwardine, a Chancellor and Treasurer of England, and his love of books became so famous that he was reported "to burn with such a desire for books and especially old ones that it was more easy for any man to gain our favour by means of books than of money. The aumbries of the most famous monasteries were thrown open, cases were unlocked and caskets were undone, and volumes that had slumbered through long ages in their tombs wake up and are astonished." The great discoverer's pleasure at the university of Paris corresponds to that of visitors to Oxford in later years. "There," he says, "are delightful libraries, more aromatic than stores of spicery; there are luxuriant parks of all manner of volumes; there are Academic meads shaken by the tramp of scholars; there are lounges of Athens; walks of the Peripatetics; peaks of Parnassus; and porches of the Stoics. There is seen the surveyor of all Arts and Sciences, Aristotle, to whom belongs all that is most excellent in doctrine, so far as relates to this passing sublunary world; there Ptolemy measures epicycles and eccentric apogees and the nodes of the planets by figures and numbers; there Paul reveals the mysteries." And to complete the resemblance of Oxford to such a place, he gave all his books to "our hall at Oxford," where the masters and scholars were to pray for his soul. The fate of his collection may have been worthy, but is mysterious. It is said to have been divided, and part of it perhaps went to Balliol. It could have found no more honourable abode than the Balliol library. From the beginning gifts of books had come in, but chiefly what was even then old-fashioned, until the middle of the fifteenth century. It was the period when Guarino at Ferrara was an inspiration to Europe. Robert Fleming was one of his pupils, and sent beautiful manuscripts to Lincoln College library; and at Lincoln books flowed in before cash. Three others of Guarino's pupils were Balliol men : Gray, Bishop of Ely and Chancellor of the University, whose books were collected with Guarino's help, and passed, the finest of their day, to Balliol at his death ; Free, public reader of physic at Ferrara, a great benefactor of libraries, and a historian of trees and plants ; and Tiptoft, Earl of Worcester, splendid, eloquent, cruel ; who had made golden speeches to the Pope, the Cardinals, the men of Padua ; had translated Cicero ; and on his return, adorned England with his learning and patronage, and shocked it with the refined cruelties of Italy. His collection of manuscripts went with Duke Humphrey's to the University library, where a room was made for them, over the quiet Divinity School then being built between St. Mary's and Durham Hall. Tiptoft was the most striking type of the Renaissance, of English blood. But it was the Italian Renaissance; and after his death the direct influence of Italy was small in Oxford.

It was, however, an Italian, Vitelli, who uttered the first words of Greek in Oxford. Plato was soon to enjoy a new life there, and to be woven into the past of Oxford, as if he had really been of its children. *It comes et paribus curis vestigia figit.* It was an age of great, unpopular men who came and went suddenly and obscurely in Oxford, like the first lecturers of the twelfth century. They were divinely inflated with the beauty of Greek—a language always more strange and exotic and fascinating to Englishmen than Latin—and with admiration of the restorers of that beauty, Chrysoloras, Chalcondila, Politian. Grocyn, a Magdalen man, fresh from Italy, taught Greek in the hall of Exeter. Linacre, a great physician and Grecian, was Fellow of All Souls'. The refined, persuasive Colet, whose "sacred fury" in argument Erasmus praised, was also a Magdalen man, and founder of St. Paul's school. Sir Thomas More, the most perfect, but unhappily not the most influential type of the English Renaissance, was at St. Mary Hall. Erasmus met them all in Oxford, within that old gateway of St. Mary's College in New Inn Hall Street. As they stepped out after the symposium, one pointed to a planet in the sky:

"See how Jupiter shines; it is an omen," said he.

"Yes," said another, "and we have been listening to Apollo."

For a time the Grecians were ridiculed and attacked

Oxford

in the streets by men who called themselves Priam, Hector, and Paris, and behaved—like Trojans. In that first enthusiasm men seemed very near to the inaccessible gods. Perhaps some were disposed to follow Pico della Mirandola in pursuit of them. There was therefore a party which opposed the study of Greek as heretical; and More was withdrawn from Oxford to avoid the danger.

From the beautiful Magdalen cloisters came the men who launched Corpus Christi College, just after Erasmus had published the New Testament in Greek and the ancient Brasenose Hall had at last grown into a college. The founder gave copies of Homer, Herodotus, Plato, and Horace, which still survive. There was a public lecturer in Greek on the foundation. Erasmus himself applauded and prophesied liberally of its future. It was the "new college" of the Renaissance, as Wykeham's had been of the Middle Ages. The readers were to be chosen from England or Greece or Italy. And among the first members of the college was the mystical Bavarian dialler, Nicholas Kratzer, who made a dial in Corpus garden, and that exquisite one for Wolsey, which is to be seen, in drawing, in the library. Wolsey's own college was built over against St. Frideswide's, part of which, together with one side of its cloisters, was destroyed to give it place. It contained the largest quadrangle and the most princely kitchen in Oxford. When Henry the Eighth spoiled the monasteries, the bells of Osney were carried to Christ Church; and one of them, over Wolsey's gateway, does what it can to call the undergraduates home at nine, with a deep voice, as if it spoke through its beard, which pretends to be B flat—"Bim-bom," as the old leonine hexameter says.

Hark! the bonny Christ Church bells—1, 2, 3, 4, 5, 6—
They sound so wondrous great, so wondrous sweet,
As they trowl so merrily, merrily.
Oh! the first and second bell,
That every day, at four and ten, cry,
"Come, come, come to prayers!"
And the verger troops before the Dean.
Tinkle, tinkle, ting, goes the small bell at nine,
To call the bearers home :
    But the devil a man
    Will leave his can
Till he hears the mighty Tom.

So runs the catch of a later Dean. At Christ Church also there was a lecturer in Greek. The dialler, Kratzer, was made mathematical professor. Wolsey's chapel never rose above a few feet in height, and the uncompleted walls remained for a century ; St. Frideswide's became, almost at the same time, the cathedral of the newly-created see of Oxford, and the chapel of the college.

The grandiose Christ Church kitchen, which caused so much laughter because it was the Cardinal's first contribution to his college, was in fact rather characteristic of the age that followed. It was built with the revenues of suppressed monasteries. It was almost contemporaneous with the destruction of many priceless books by reformers who were as ignorant of what is dangerous in books as a Russian censor. The shelves of Duke Humphrey's library were denuded and sold.

Oxford

The shrine of St. Frideswide's, where the University had long offered reverence twice a year, was shattered; the fragments were used here and there in the buildings of the time. The relics of the saint were husbanded by a pious few in hope of a restoration; but they were finally interred with those of Peter Martyr's wife—a significant mixture. It was the age when the University became the playground of the richer classes, and the nobleman's son took the place of the poor scholar in a fellowship. Now men found time to dispute with Cambridge as to which university was of the greatest antiquity. The arguments put forward in Oxford were seldom more convincing than this: that Oxford was named from a ford, Cambridge from a bridge; and since the ford must have been older than the bridge, Oxford was therefore founded first. Greek for the time decayed, and the founder of Trinity College feared that its restoration was impossible in that age. As to Latin, Sir Philip Sidney, who was at Christ Church, told his brother that Ciceronianism was become an abuse among the Oxonians, "who neglected things for words." Oxford was dignified mainly by the architecture of Christ Church; by the foundation of Trinity, St. John's, and Jesus College, all on learned and holy ground; by the martyrdom of Latimer and Ridley, opposite Balliol; and by great names, like those of Burton and Marston at Brasenose, Peele at Broadgates Hall (Pembroke), Raleigh at Oriel, Hooker at Corpus Christi. Religion was still in the pot, and men could not confidently tell what it would turn out to be. On the one hand,

The Stones of Oxford

the Earl of Leicester, as Chancellor of the University, mended and confirmed its organisation; on the other hand, John Lyly was "the fiddlestick of Oxford," and other Magdalen men, lovers of open air, and especially in the windy forest of Shotover, slew the King's deer. At the new college of St. John's, fellows and presidents suffered for the old religion, and Edwin Campion was hanged; they preserved, and still preserve, the statue of St. Bernard from the old foundation to which their college succeeded. At the end of the century, the most effective Oxford man of his time, William Laud, became Fellow of St. John's. He built a new quadrangle, and as Chancellor made of the statutes that long and many-tailed whip which every one knows. He created modern Broad Street by deleting the cottages which stood near and opposite to Trinity. The impressive, uncomfortable Convocation House was his work. Within sight of it was the library which Sir Thomas Bodley earlier in the century had built and stored. It became the calmest, most inviolate, and most learned place in Europe.

At Christ Church, Dean Duppa, the first of the improvers of Oxford, was beginning the work of destruction which the Puritans continued so well. But it was then the good fortune of several colleges to receive large additions of a simple and homely character, which did more than any others to make Oxford what it is. It was the age of the retired Lincoln College chapel, with its carved panels of perfumed cedar and rich, quaint glass; the placid garden front of Wadham, as seen through the cedar tree to-day; the front and colonnades of St. John's which look on the garden ; the south end of the Exeter garden front that sees so much ; the front quadrangle of University College ; the hall and chapel of St. Mary's Hall ; the east end of Jesus College chapel, which was just finished when Henry Vaughan arrived ; and the front quadrangle of Pembroke College, converted from Broadgates Hall by a clothier, the Earl of Pembroke, and James I., and opened with ceremonies which included a fantastic Latin oration by Sir Thomas Browne, as senior undergraduate. The architecture of Wadham is a remarkable proof of the influence of antiquity upon men and things in Oxford. The founders, in 1609, were Nicholas Wadham and Dorothy, his wife, of Merifield in Somerset. The builders were mainly west country men, and worked in that lingering Gothic style which was still vital in Oxford, and seems to have guided the hand of Wren (if it was Wren) when he planned the fan tracery of Brasenose chapel. But in the building of Wadham chapel, one John Spicer and his men seem to have been haunted by the beauty of the Perpendicular churches of their native Somerset. The windows are so clear a reconstruction of this dream that an experienced judge refused to believe that they were of later date than Christ Church. Thither came a son of Sir Walter Raleigh and Robert Blake, who took opposite sides when the Civil War broke out.

There was a prelusive struggle between town and gown in the year before the war. The chancellorship of Laud had roused opposition ; but the University was almost unanimous for Charles, and easily chose its side, when he demanded a loan on the eve of the war.

Van Ling had just painted the windows of University College chapel. The Dean of Christ Church, or rather "Smith of London," had just finished the airy over-traceried approach to Christ Church hall, upon which every one looks back as he steps down to the cloisters. Other work was in preparation at Christ Church. But all building suddenly ceased.

A brief visit of Parliament troops to the yet unfortified city was recorded by the shattering of the Virgin and her Child over St. Mary's porch. After Edgehill, the King came to Oxford, and the effect was worse than the mutilation of a Virgin of stone. The University Volunteers, some armed with bows, were drilled in the quadrangle of New College and Christ Church, and skirmished in the Parks. The royal artillery lay in Magdalen Grove. New College tower and cloisters became the arsenal : New Inn Hall the mint. Charles and Queen Henrietta Maria were lodged at Merton. The Court was held at Christ Church. A Fellow of Magdalen and a Fellow of All Souls' edited the royalist gazette, *Mercurius Aulicus*, "the latter pleasing more with his buffoneries." The besieging Parliamentarians were spread about the high ground of Headington, and the low fields on the north of the city.

The greater number of scholars left Oxford, and their rooms were occupied by ladies and cavaliers. College trees were cut down for use in the defences.

Oxford

A little war, much gallantry and coarseness, drove away learning and tranquillity, unwilling to linger for the sound of Sir John Denham's smooth and insipid Muse, which produced *Cooper's Hill* in 1642. The Muses were probably in hiding abroad with Lovelace and Marvell; for Milton was writing only prose, and George Wither, a Magdalen man, was a captain of Parliamentary horse at Maidstone. Yet a contemporary pamphlet says that "Robin Goodfellow" found the Muses near Eynsham. "He had not gone as far as Ensham, but he espied the nine Muses in a vintner's porch crouching close together, and defending themselves as well as they could from the cold visitation of the winter's night. They were extream poore, and (which is most strange) in so short an absence and distance from Oxford they were grown extreamly ignorant, for they took him for their Apollo, and craved his power and protection to support them."

One room at Trinity College was pleasant still; for the glass of the window was richly painted with a St. Gregory. And there Aubrey received the newly-published *Religio Medici*, "which first opened my understanding." He carried it to Eston with Sir Kenelm Digby. Coming back to Oxford, he bade a servant to draw the ruins of Osney "two or three ways before 'twas pulled down."

Plague came in 1643, fire in the following year. The Cavaliers were reputed to have embezzled books from the Bodleian, which had formerly resisted, and won the respect of, Charles himself. The colleges made what some call a "friendly loan" of all their plate : it was never returned or replaced by the King. Week by week, they furnished him with labour and cash. And when the Parliamentarians entered at last, there were at Merton, for example, "no Bachelors, hardly any Scholars, and few Masters," and the hall was untenantable. The triumph of Parliament brought with it an inquisition in Oxford, which resulted in the exile, not without force, of the greater number of heads of houses and fellows for refusal to submit. The soldiers broke the Magdalen chapel window-glass ; Cromwell himself took away the college organ to Hampton Court. But "the first thing General Fairfax did, was to set a good guard of soldiers to preserve the Bodleian Library. He was a lover of learning, and had he not taken this special care, that noble library had been utterly destroyed." The chief objection to the intruded fellows and heads of houses seems to have been that they were intruded and were likely to stay. As for their accomplishments, though some lacked humour, they seem to have been respectable. The undergraduates and bachelors were in the main loyal to Cromwell ; and when Prince Charles was rumoured to be approaching Oxford, New College tower became a Parliament citadel, and a troop of horse was enlisted from the colleges. The old glory of religion faded ; the sound of distant Latin chanted was no longer heard in Christ Church and New College. But in one house, three devoted men preserved the old religion right through the Commonwealth, constantly and without molestation. Other changes made men more content. Three coffee-houses were opened in Oxford and patronised by royalists and "others who esteemed themselves virtuosi and wits." Men who would have adorned any age came up. Christopher Wren came to Wadham, and thence to All Souls'. Evelyn revisited Oxford and found no just ground to regret the former times, . . . "creation of Doctors, by the cap, ring, kiss, etc., those ancient ceremonies and institutions, as yet not wholly abolished." At All Souls' he heard "music, voices, and theorbos, performed by some ingenious scholars." At New College "the chapel was in its ancient garb, notwithstanding the scrupulosity of the times," and the chapel at Magdalen was "in pontificial order, the altar only I think turned table-wise." Then he dined at Wadham, and wrote down an account of what he saw at the Warden's, "that most obliging and universally curious Dr. Wilkins." The transparent apiaries, hollow speaking statues, dials, waywisers, and other "artificial mathematical and magical curiosities," which he saw, well illustrate the activities of the time in the cradle of the Royal Society.

A little after Wren came Thomas Traherne, the poet, to Brasenose, still enjoying that childhood which he praised so adeptly. We may think of him in the peaceful embowered city as having that characteristic ecstasy at the sight of common things which his lyrical prose describes. "The corn was orient and immortal wheat which never should be reaped nor was ever sown. I thought it had stood from everlasting to everlasting. The dust and stones of the street were as precious as gold : the gates were at first the end of the world. The green trees, when I saw them first through one of the gates, transported and ravished me ; their sweetness and unusual beauty made my heart to leap, and almost mad with ecstasy, they were such strange and wonderful things. The men ! O what venerable and reverend creatures did the aged men seem ! Immortal cherubim ! And young men glittering and sparkling angels, and maids strange seraphic pieces of life and beauty ! "

Again, books began to flow in their natural courses to the libraries. Selden's eight thousand came to the Bodleian. Building was resumed ; for Brasenose chapel was half built by the time of the Restoration.

The Restoration restored to Oxford the Church, a few excellent old men, and the morals of the siege. The august Clarendon was indeed Chancellor ; but the city became a fashionable resort. Charles II., with his Queen and Castlemaine, were there in 1663, and again with the Parliament in the year of the plague. " High-thundering Jove," runs a contemporary ballad, supposed to be spoken by London to Oxford :—

> High-thundering Jove cannot withstand thy charms,
> That Britain's mighty monarch in thy arms
> Canst hold so fast, and quite to overcome
> The greatest potentate in Christendom.

The aim of scholars, said Anthony à Wood, " is not to live as students ought to do, viz., temperate, abstemious, and plain and grave in their apparel ; but to live like gentry, to keep dogs and horses, to turn their studies into places to keep bottles, to swagger in gay apparell and long periwigs!" There was too much punning, thought Eachard. In his inquiry into the causes of the contempt of the clergy, he is not kind to the University of the day, and asks, "Whether or not Punning, Quibbling, and that which they call Joquing, and such delicacies of wit, highly admired in some academic exercises, might not be very conveniently omitted?" The first Common Room was established at Merton soon after the Restoration. But in that age even Common Rooms seem to have been but privileged and secluded inns, and quite without the severely genial amphictyonic character of to-day. When Pepys visited Oxford he naturally found it "a very sweet place"; spent 2s. 6d. on a barber in its honour; 10s. "to him that showed us All Souls' College and Chichley's picture"; 2s. for seeing the Brasenose butteries and the gigantic hand of the "Child of Hale"; and having seen the Physic Garden, the hospital, and Friar Bacon's study, concluded: "Oxford mighty fine place, well seated, and cheap entertainment." But the cheap entertainment is now among the lost causes. A little while afterwards, Evelyn attended the opening of the Sheldonian Theatre, built by Wren. He complained of the "tedious, abusive, sarcastical rhapsody" which was permitted on that occasion to the *Terræ Filius*, a kind of Billingsgate Aristophanes, who half-officially represented the undergraduate aversion to sweetness and light. The university printing-office lay under the theatre, and, says a ballad of the time—

> What structure else but prides it to reveal
> Treasures ? which bashful this would fain conceal ; . . .
> Spain, Gascoin, Florence, Smyrna, and the Rhine
> May taste their language there, tho' not the wine.
> The Jew, Mede, Edomite, Arabian, Crete,
> In those deep vaults their wandring ideoms meet,
> And to compute, are in amazement hurld,
> How long since Oxford has been all the world.

At Magdalen, men were planting the elms of the grove and laying out the walks round the meadow. Bishop Fell was completing the west front of Christ Church, which the Civil War had interrupted, and planting those elms in the Broad Walk that look on the Cathedral and Corpus and Merton, and, farther off, Magdalen tower. In 1680 Wren's tower over Wolsey's gateway at Christ Church was finished. One of the Osney bells was recast to hang therein.

The resistance of James II. fell in this coarse, frivolous, self-satisfied age. He was welcomed to Oxford by music and ceremony. The conduit "ran claret for the vulgar." But when he adventured to force his nominee into the presidentship of Magdalen, he could not even procure a blacksmith to burst a resisting door. Again, the University stood to arms to oppose Monmouth's rebellion, and clothed its members in scarlet coats, with scarves, and white-plumed hats ; but had to be contented with the bonfires in celebration of the victory at Sedgemoor, and a full-dress parade. Not long afterwards many yards of orange ribbon made the High Street gaudy with a pretence at honouring William III. But the colleges were vigorously Jacobite, and proved it by drinking the healths of the Stuarts as long as they could. Merton, Exeter, All Souls', and Wadham were the exceptions. One example of the lighter occupations of the period is to be found in a story of somewhat earlier date, told of Dr. Bathurst, Vice-Chancellor and President of Trinity. "A striking instance of zeal for his college, in the dotage of old age, is yet remembered. Balliol College had suffered so much in the outrages of the grand rebellion, that it remained almost in a state of desolation for some years after the Restoration, a circumstance not to be suspected from its flourishing condition ever since. Dr. Bathurst was perhaps secretly pleased to see a neighbouring and once rival society reduced to this condition, while his flourished beyond all others. Accordingly, one afternoon, he was found in his garden, which then ran almost continuous to the east side of Balliol College, throwing stones at the windows with much satisfaction, as if happy to contribute his share in completing the appearance of its ruin." I seem to find an echo of the sentiment of very different men, with a love of the old time amidst the politics and wine of the day, in Aubrey's ejaculation : he wished that monasteries had not entirely been suppressed ; for if but a few had been left, "what a pleasure 'twould have been to have travelled from monastery to monastery!" Nevertheless, the Oxford output of bishops was not decreased, and the number of quiet scholars—men like

The Stones of Oxford

Hody of Wadham—was larger than one might conclude from the pages of *honest* Thomas Hearne, of St. Edmund Hall.

It was upon an old monastic foundation — once Gloucester College, then Gloucester Hall — that the one new eighteenth - century college was established. Gloucester Hall had numbered among its inhabitants several famous, rather odd men, like Tom Coryat and Thomas Allen, but had fallen away after the Restoration. It was, in short, almost a possession of nettles. The buildings were only kept on the edge of desolation by the Principal and two or three families in residence. The seventeenth century had made one fantastic attempt to retrieve the Hall. A colony of twenty students from the four Patriarchates of the Eastern Church was to be regularly established there. But the dreamy plan was soon parched and destroyed in the odour of scandal. After much trifling procrastination, the Greeks were succeeded by Worcester College, and a lucky poverty left the worn old buildings for a little longer untroubled. A library, a hall, and a chapel were prepared for the new society. Wide spaces of land on every side of it were retained or acquired, which afterwards gave the college a fat rent and its incomparable bosky and watered garden.

While Worcester was being founded in the conventional way, Oxford was developed by such buildings as the cloister at Corpus, the Pembroke chapel, the hall at All Souls', the front quadrangle at Queen's, and the little Lincoln "Grove" cottages. Then also the

Oxford

Trinity College lime trees were planted. In most of the work of that time Dean Aldrich of Christ Church had a hand or a word. This clever and genial tutor was one of the best men of his day, and quite typical of the early eighteenth century. He seems to have been one to whom action came more naturally than dreams, if he dreamed at all; and he could easily express the many sides of his personality in a lasting way. A happy and golden mediocrity! He encouraged Boyle in the dazzling indiscretion of *The Epistles of Phalaris*. He wrote the enduring Oxford Logic, a smoking catch, and "Hark! the bonny Christ Church bells"; and perhaps this translation :—

> If on my theme I rightly think,
> There are five reasons why men drink,
> Good wine, a friend, or being dry,
> Or lest we should be, by and by,
> Or any other reason why.

The size of his architectural designs is seen in Peckwater quadrangle at Christ Church; their charm, in All Saints', which the moon loves. Soon after his death in 1710, the stately library at Christ Church and that copious one at All Souls' were begun.

In the year of the building of Pembroke chapel, Samuel Johnson entered the college, where they preserve his deal writing-table and china tea-pot. As Aldrich represents the early part of the century in Oxford, so Johnson represents the middle. Men are nowadays disposed to blame the cheerfulness of an age that produced a hundred immortals who do not give the true ring. The college historians often entitle one of their eighteenth - century chapters the "dark" or "iron" age ; and indeed, as a "school of universal learning," the Oxford of that day might be called in question. It was more aristocratic and exclusive, perhaps, than it had ever been, and it failed to justify itself. "What class in life"—it was a song by a fellow in a play of the period—

> What class in life, tho' ne'er so great,
> With a good fellowship can compare ?

And in the same play, says one, of Horace, "He was a jolly *utile dulci* dog, and I believe formerly might be fellow at a college." Yet in our backward glances over Oxford history, how often do we stop when we reach that age ! whether we are drinking from an old reminding tankard with the date 17—, or looking at one of its books, or living in one of the rooms which it wainscotted or furnished, heavily but how genially ! "You are a philosopher, Dr. Johnson," said Edwards, his college friend. "I have tried too in my time to be a philosopher ; but I don't know how, cheerfulness was always breaking in." Cheerfulness broke in pretty often in Oxford. And that was a time when there was more love of Oxford than ever before. Even the wealthy Fellows of All Souls' ("that Eden to the fruitful mind," as Lady Winchilsea called it at that time) never bought their college ; and when one of them was taunted with the quip that Oxford was less learned than Bath, he was able to reply that it was also more fashionable. I find, too, in its love of the past, as

Oxford

in its love of nature, something heartier, though I dare-say less mystical, than our own. Johnson's love of Pembroke is an example. He had lived there as an undergraduate only fourteen months, and there seems to have been little that was tangible, to take hold of him in so short a time. Yet when he came back long after, and heard old Camden's grace after meat—which they still use—he was at home. It is true that men of that age could as little appreciate its blank verse as we can compose it, but there were many who could then appreciate what we can now only describe. The country (in summer)—antiquity—good living—were fine things; but when they wrote, it was theology, or morals, or in-accurate philology. There was a man, long ago with God, who after much waiting obtained a fine coveted room at New College : instead of writing a sonnet forthwith, he expressed a wish to kick some one downstairs inconti-nently. On one occasion, it is said, the head of a college, and a great lover of Oxford, who was jocund and recumbent after a feast, was with great circumstance invited by several wags " to accept the crown of this old and famous kingdom, since King George has resigned." To which he slowly replied, without surprise, that " if we can hold our Court of St. James's in this Common Room, we shall not demur." Warton's *Companion to the Guide* and Wood's *Modius Salium* are full of what we should call poor Oxford humour ; but I think there is sufficient indication of the laughter it caused, to make us pause in any condemnation of it as compared with our own "thoughtful mirth," which

The Stones of Oxford

inspires mainly a desire to say something more mirthful and less thoughtful. And for those who care for none of these things, what sweeter or more dignified picture of quietness and study is there than at Lincoln in Wesley's time, or at University under Scott, or Christ Church under Jackson? What handsomer than the Camera which was built in the middle of that century, or better to live in than Fisher's buildings at Balliol? Or what inheritance more agreeable than the old bowling-greens, so happily celebrated in the Sphæristerium; or than the college gardens, which are nearly all eighteenth-century gifts? It has been said that the only movement in the eighteenth century was a very slow ascent to the nineteenth. That is not quite so, as many will agree who look at the re-fronting of University College chapel and hall, which was done when the wonderful century was reached at length. In fact, if we condemn the eighteenth century, we have to disown a large part of the nineteenth. In Oxford that is especially so. The destruction of the old chapels at Balliol and Exeter, and of the Grove at Merton, was carried out not much more than fifty years ago; so long have the dark ages lingered in Oxford. As for the new buildings at New College, Christ Church, Merton, etc., they have been so widely condemned that it is to be presumed there is some merit in them, which an age nearer the millennium will praise.

But those works are only the less admirable and more conspicuous emblems of the nineteenth-century reformation. It had at length become possible again for a man to keep his terms and take his degree without continual residence within college walls. The numbers of the University grew rapidly, and at a time when more efficient tutors and discipline made Oxford attractive to many who were neither frivolous nor rich. Oxford became, in fact, a place of education. The previous century had been conspicuous for great names and lack of system ; what was achieved was due to individual endowment and energy ; and the able men stood somewhat apart from their contemporaries. Wesley, for example, not only failed to make a strong party, but even to rouse an opposition of useful size. The nineteenth century, on the other hand, was a sociable one in matters of intellect. There were few lonely names. There were many groups. College after college—in a few cases before, in nearly all cases after, the first Commission—became known for their style of thought more than for their noblemen or wine. The fault of monkishness was either blotted out or exchanged for one that is more commonly pardoned to-day, *nimium gaudens popularibus auris*. At first, this meant an emphasis upon the distinction between college and college. It required more than a walk up Turl Street to get from Oriel to Balliol. The competition engendered by the new separate honour schools probably increased this for a time ; and it was reported of one Head that, when told that Worcester College was above his own in a class list, he turned to the butler, and asked where Worcester was. But the east wind of the Commission changed all that. At the same time

The Stones of Oxford

the friendly and often stimulating intercourse between senior and junior members of the colleges grew apace, and was no doubt encouraged by the increasing fashionableness of athletic sports, which gave a " Blue " the importance of a fellow, and a greater consciousness of importance.

In its progress towards what is most admired in modern Oxford, Balliol is the most interesting college. Nearly all other colleges have indeed acquired a more or less thorough resemblance to Balliol in its good and bad points, but no other college has been so long, so persistently, and so progressively devoted to the same ideal. Even those who do not wholly like that ideal cannot fail to admire the consistency and energy of the men who have achieved it, or could find the like to any comparable extent in colleges that cherish other affections.

But nowhere has there been an entire rupture with the past, or anything new which has not in a sense been laid reverently upon the foundations of the old. If one could see Keble College without its buildings, it might well seem to be not the youngest of the colleges. So, too, with Hertford College, which is indeed but the rejuvenation of the old homes of Hobbes, Selden, and Matthew Hale : it has doffed knee-breeches and periwig, and even those perhaps unwillingly, since its fellowships are lifelong for the celibate. And in the architecture of Oxford, some of the most novel effects of last century were produced by work in the same spirit of reverence for the past. Here, a window received back its casements again ; there, a fine roof was rescued from its burial under the impertinent superimpositions of more egotistic innovators. No other age and city perhaps would have been so curious and fortunate in restoring the old, as when at Christ Church the old floral marble base of St. Frideswide's shrine was restored after three hundred years in the wilderness. Part was found in the cemetery wall, part in a well-side, part in a staircase, part in a wall : and almost the whole now rests in the Cathedral again.

DONS ANCIENT AND MODERN

CHAPTER III

DONS ANCIENT AND MODERN

MODERN

THE senior members of the University are perhaps as interesting as they have ever been. The freshman or other critical stranger to the city finds them less picturesque, if his ideal be anything like that of the youthful Ruskin, who looked for presences like the Erasmus of Holbein or Titian's Magnificoes, and was disappointed at Christ Church by all save one. For the President or Master, whose absolutism used to be the envy of kings, now bears his honours inconspicuously. The fellows of colleges are no longer, indeed, a distinct and noticeable class, but are, for the most part, purely and simply scholars, or historians, or instructors of youth. The conscientious, capable, and hard-working Don is probably commoner than he has ever been; and his success is great. But even he might echo the cry against a possible tendency towards mere educational efficiency in fellows, which is expressed in the exclamation : " Nothing is so much to be feared

71

as that we should one day compete with the Elementary Schools."

"O goodly usage of those antique times," when it was a sufficient grace to be a scholar, and it was a kind of virtue to quote from Horace and never to play upon words outside Homer. Here and there such a man survives, always old, married to the place, and yet with a widowed air, looking as if he had crept out of one of the reverend pictures in the hall, and still clear-sighted enough to see the length of Broad Street and regret it, fumbling with the spectacles which he bought to protect his eyes in the first year of railway travelling. No one could draw him quite so happily as the Sub-Rector of Lincoln College, and in his latest book he gives us a charming hint, and there, quite appropriately, but too pathetically, he allows the old scholar to die.

"The Church, indeed," he writes, "was mouldy enough, and the air within was close and sleep-giving ; and as the old parson murmured his sermon twice a Sunday from the high old pulpit, his hearers gradually dropped into a tranquil doze or a pleasant day-dream— all except the old Scholar, who sat just below, holding his hand to his ear, and eagerly looking for one of those subtle allusions, those reminiscences of old reading, or even now and then three words of Latin from Virgil or the *Imitatio* with which his lifelong friend would strain a point to please him. They had been at school together, and at college together, and now they were spending their last years together, for the old Scholar had come, none of us knew whence, and settled down in the manor-house by the churchyard, hard by the Rectory of his old companion. And so they walked together through the still shady avenues of life's evening, wishing for no change, reading much and talking little, lovers of old times and old books, seeking the truth, not indeed in the world around them, but in the choice words of the wise men of old : *Pia et humilis inquisitio veritatis per sanas patrum sententias studens ambulare.*

I

Such a one there was, until recently, to be met walking on a fine day between Magdalen and Oriel ; or even, in April, as far as the Shotover road in expectation of hearing the nightingales ; or as far as Carfax to learn whether the tower was looking any older. He was exquisitely courteous, without a tinge of mere courtliness, and could hate and contemn. Such was his loathing of what was unseemly that he begged he might be awakened by any one that heard him snore. If he was a misogynist, it was because he was shy and ignorant of women. He would gently insinuate, and as if it were temerity, that even good women cannot distinguish between fiction and Jane Austen, and have been known to deposit pins in ashtrays. He could not express an opinion upon subjects which he ignored or disliked, and when they were discussed in the Common Room, he had an irrepressible sympathy with both sides. Thus he was no politician, but was at one with members of Parliament of both sides, by means of a little genial commonplace. But on his hobby-horses—*sublimis in equis*—he had a sweet eloquence which he "hoped was not persuasive." For he disliked proselytisers more than proselytes. In later years, he became too deaf to be quite honest in answering a stupid or knavish man. He had, too, a little vocal impediment which he could use rhetorically. Preaching one day at a country church, he was dwelling at length upon the good qualities of a prophet.

"That's parson all over," murmured now and then a grey parishioner, and inquired of whom he spoke.

"Isaiah or Habakkuk," explained his neighbour.

"Then I don't believe," answered the disappointed man, "there is such a person—unless 'tis another name for parson."

When an old lady lay a-dying, and was troubled concerning the destiny of her magpie and tame hare after her death, the curate amiably suggested that Providence would take care of them.

"No, no," she interposed, "give them to Mr. ——."

He was, despite features which the dull might call plain, remarkably, and I had almost said physically, beautiful, because of the clear shining of his character. The tender motives that often moulded his lips, the purity and grace that found expression in his eyes, and that fluctuation of the lines of the face in thought which is almost light and shade, wrought an immortal beauty out of Nature's poor endowment. Nor was that only when he was in a fit small company. Some men, when

Dons Ancient and Modern

not moved by such an influence, lapse into that sculptured and muddy expression which is the chief quality of photographs. You may surprise them void and waste. But if he was ever surprised, it might be seen that he turned to the intruder fresh from a spiritual colloquy. His smile, on opening Plutarch, was as if he blessed and was blessed, and restored the beholder to the age of the first revival of learning. Very soft—some said mincing—was his step among his books, as not knowing what or whom he might disturb. If you saw him in the Bodleian, he seemed its familiar spirit, and in some way its outward and visible expression or heraldic device. Though a wide and learned reader, he had published nothing that had anything to do with books. In his youth he had circulated " An Elegy written within sight of Keble College," and in later years speculations on the Jurassic sea and the migration of birds. He often read aloud to himself, and even to others on being provoked, in his sounding wainscotted room in sight of All Saints steeple. Especially he liked to chant Sophocles, and to the opening of *Electra* gave a solemn and almost religious sweetness in the rendering. Then it was that we knew how he had gained and preserved that notable grace of pronunciation. He used to say, " It is a fine day," instead of " Tserfineday." And thus of every day he made a rosary of gracious thoughts and deeds among men and Nature and books ; and apparelling a worldly life with the sanctity of unworldly temperance and charity, his homeliness became dignified without

75

Oxford drawl. His sitting-room is magnificent, and like style, conceals the man. It is no wonder that a man with such arm-chairs should be well satisfied. His books are noble up to the year 1800—abundant and select, often old, always fine; but after the year 1800 a certain timidity of taste may be observed. Of course his friends' books are there, with the books which you are expected to know in country houses. For the rest, he has overcome the difficulty of selection by not selecting. As the college has good port and is in-different in its choice of white wine, so he has good classics and a jumble of later work. He is charitable, a ready contributor to approved causes. He has travelled, and is never reduced to silence in company. He is a good talker, knowing how not to offend. He is a brilliant host, suave, considerate,—with comprehensive views,—and ready to make allowances for those who are not Dons. Perhaps he is in the main a summer bird. Then he shows that he is a gallant as well as a scholar and man of the world. He is the figure-head of his college barge during The Eights, and with an eye-glass, that is a kind of sixth sense, he surveys womankind, and sees that it is good.

III

There was lately also a more Roman type amongst us. He had a lusty Terentian wit that was not in the fashion of these times; and his proud frankness about everything but his soul found even less welcome from a generation that liked to talk of little else. " A little hypocrisy "—such was his advice to freshmen, but not his practice—" a little hypocrisy is useful to a virtuous man, since it is hard not to appear a hypocrite, especially when one is not." He was what is called an intemperate man. For, though a small, fastidious eater and short sleeper, he was a man of many bottles ; nor had he the common gift of repenting of the truths which claret inspired and port enabled him to express. He never learned to whine over private infelicity — a weighty shortcoming ; or to moralise on the infelicities of others —which was almost a virtue. A small Kantian once asked him how he felt after a bereavement. " It has never occurred to me," was his reply, " to think how I felt." An unsuccessful man himself, and burdened by his more successful and more indolent relatives, his catchword was, nevertheless, " Success." But he perhaps hated more than a noisy failure a noisy success. Always scheming on behalf of others, he laid no plans for himself, except by writing his own epitaph, on the day before his death. He ate, drank, was merry, and did his duty. He was the life and soul and financial saviour of his college. At no time was he a profound student ; he had been elected to a fellowship on account of his birth ; yet the brilliant scholar and the nice courtier of the college admitted that he, the chapel, and the cook were equally indispensable. In fact, he was as near to the ideal head of a college as it would be wise to have in an ancient university. He could not lecture, and was a poor judge of imitation Greek prose. He radiated

Dons Ancient and Modern

a clean and vigorous worldly influence through both Common Rooms. He knew every undergraduate who was within the reach of knowledge. His judgment of men was as consummate and as untransferable as his judgment of wine. It was his custom to say that there had been three philosophers, two ancient, one modern, in the history of the world—Ecclesiastes, Democritus, and Sir William Temple of Moor Park. To his pupils he used to pronounce that, "since you are average men and will never be able to understand Ecclesiastes or take the trouble to understand Democritus," they should follow the Englishman. He then repeated from memory this passage (with such solemnity that I believe he felt it to be his own):—

"Some writers, in casting up the goods most desirable in life, have given them this rank—health, beauty, and riches. Of the first, I find no dispute ; but to the two others much may be said ; for beauty is a good that makes others happy rather than one's self ; and how riches should claim so high a rank I cannot tell, when so great, so wise, and so good a part of mankind have, in all ages, preferred poverty before them—the Therapeutae and Ebionites among the Jews, the primitive monks and modern friars among Christians, so many dervises among the Mahometans, the Brachmans among the Indians, and all the ancient philosophers ; who, whatever else they differed in, agreed in this, of despising riches, and at best esteeming them an unnecessary trouble or encumbrance of life : so that whether they are to be reckoned among goods or evils, is yet left in doubt.

79

Oxford

"When I was young, and in some idle company, it was proposed that every one should tell what their three wishes should be, if they were sure to be granted : some were very pleasant, and some very extravagant ; mine were health, and peace, and fair weather ; which, though out of the way among young men, yet perhaps might pass well enough among old : they are all of a strain ; for health in the body is like peace in the state, and serenity in the air ; the sun, in our climate at least, has something so reviving, that a fair day is a kind of sensual pleasure, and of all others the most innocent."

The last words he would often repeat, with this comment : that people to-day were so much busied with sunsets and landscapes and colours that they had no such hearty feeling for Nature as the old seventeenth-century statesman, philosopher, and gardener had.

"Read Cowley and Pope," was his only criticism in English literature. "Any one can be a Keats, though few can write as well," he argued, "but it is not so easy to be like Pope." Meeting Browning one day, and telling him that he enjoyed some of his poetry, the poet asked him whether he understood it. "No," said the Don, "do you?"

For twenty years, when men spoke of —— College, they thought of him. "The University of Oxford," said an old pupil who lived to send his son to that college, "the University of Oxford, at least as a place of education, consists of old ——, the river, and the college pump." That college is now like Roman

Dons Ancient and Modern

literature without Lucretius, or a wine-glass of cold water.

When I look back and see him, more military than ecclesiastical (except for a snuffle) in his doctorial scarlet, I think that it was partly his brow that was his power. It was a calm, ample, antique brow. In the ancient world the brow made the man and the god. It was as divine as ægis or thunder or eagle. It was more magisterial than the fasces. It commanded the Consulate and troubled the dominion of Persia and cast down the power of Hannibal. The brow of Jupiter—of Plato—of Augustus—was a hill of majesty equal with Olympus. The history of old sculpture is an *Ave!* to the brow. Now the soul has descended to the eyes. In politics, war, literature, above all in finance, victory is with the eyes. The old man had the godlike span of curving bone ; but his eyes slept. It was his good fortune and Oxford's honour that he ruled an Oxford college.

IV

Among the younger men is one who spent perhaps a year in trying to combine high living and high thinking ; then made a compromise by dropping the high thinking ; and at last, perhaps as the result of some solemn intervention, became ascetic. He is a friend of authors and potentates. He understands a bishop, and takes a kindly interest in east-enders, so long as they are in Oxford. His aspect is grave and calm, since life, in losing half its vices, has lost all its charm. Like fine cutlery, his manners lack nothing but originality ; he has a good taste in flowers, and can even arrange them. Nor is the taste in books limited by his connoisseurship in binding.   He is a free and fearless reader, yet careful in the choice of books to be left on the table.   If style were finish, his writing would be famous ; but his beautiful style is always subordinated to a really beautiful handwriting.   His originally dilettante interest in palæography has lured him into some genuine research among old manuscripts.   His lectures are therefore fresh, thoughtful, and perfect in gesture, delivery, and composition.   I seem to behold Virgil himself at the end of one of his descants, or Politian at least.   If he had not more love of the applause of his most graceful pupils than of the learned world, he might be renowned. But he is content to be three-quarters of a specialist in history and more than one of the arts, and to be a lode-star to the ladies of his audience.   Perhaps only they can do him justice.

V

There is (or was) to be found at the top of a mouldy Oxford staircase the most unpedantic man in the world, seated underneath and upon and amidst innumerable books.   In the more graceful than sufficient garments of his leisure, he looked like Homer, with hair still un-grizzled.   He spoke, and back came the *Iliad* and the *Odyssey* on that stormy sound.   But he could so well dissemble this physical magnificence that he passed in

Dons Ancient and Modern

different clothing for an able-bodied seaman and a member of Parliament.

He loved the forest and cloud and sea as if they had been brothers. To visit him in his ancient room was to take a journey to Nature : to walk with him, in all weathers—to Wood Eaton, Sunningwell, Fyfield, Northmoor—was to go with a talking and genial embodiment of the north-west wind and a dash of orchard scent.

His room was alive with the spirit of old histories. Famous men—Pericles or Alexander or John XXII.—seemed to live once more when they were discoursed of in that eloquent chamber. It may have been illusion,—for there was little talk of historical principles,—but on leaving him, a man felt that he had gone away "before the mysteries," and that if he could but live in the rooms of Urbanus, the past would be wonderfully revealed. Then, a day or two afterwards, he could remember only Urbanus himself, and, after a brief indignation at the cheiromancy quite unwittingly practised, admitted that that was sufficient.

I am not sure whether he professed history or divinity or Chinese. He wrote, however, an epoch-making treatise on "The Literature of Aboriginal Races, with special reference to Sumatra"; an invaluable brochure on "The Jewellery of the Visigothic Kings"; "A Complete Exposition of the Ancient Game of Tabblisk"; and "A Brief Summary of the Loves of Diarmad O'Diubhne." His sonnet to M. Mallarmé, though it has been described as *trop mallarmisé*, is justly admired. But he did not write ten volumes of reminiscences.

I can see him, in a brown library or a pictured hall, beginning a lecture. He moves about a little uneasily, like the late William Morris, and as if he would rather use deeds than words. An old book lies open before him : now and then he turns over a page, reads to himself, and smiles. The conscientious undergraduate looks at his watch and begins spoiling his pen upon the blotting-paper. He comes to take notes ; but Urbanus does not care. Suddenly the lecturer laughs heartily at a good passage and begins :—

"I think perhaps you will like this story . . ."

And he reads, punctuating the matter with his own lively appreciation. Somerville and Lady Margaret and St. Hugh's look resigned ; future first (or third) class men look contemptuous ; a Blue feels that his time is being wasted,—he must complain,—he rises and walks out as Urbanus remarks :—

"I don't know your name, sir, but you can sleep *here*, if you wish."

Urbanus closes the book five minutes before or after the appointed hour ; some one mutters about " the worst lecturer in this incubator of bad lecturers " : such is his influence, not so much injecting knowledge as dredging and maturing what is already gained, that others can think of him easily as a humanist of the great days, who has survived in his old college, with an indifference to mere time which is not incredible in Oxford, where memories three centuries old are still alive in oral tradition.

Dons Ancient and Modern

VI

Philip Amberley, late fellow of ——, took it much to heart that he was not born in 1300. He would have been a monk, and would have illuminated Ovid to the astonishment of all ages. All he could do in this age was to perform his tutorial duty, and to write a few pages of noble English in a caligraphy that was worthy of the ages he loved. He wrote but one book, which he burned, because nobody would give him £5 for it. A not very old or very credible story tells how an intelligent alien blurted out the question, at the high table of Philip's college : Whether the uncomely heads before the Sheldonian Theatre were not the fellows of that same college. The inquirer was corrected with asperity ; and in revenge he always stated that he afterwards received photographs of the younger fellows, by way of removing the mote from his eye. But Philip sent a photograph of the least human physiognomy, signed with full name and college. For the rest, he had that uncertainty of character which is called conscience in the good and timidity in the bad, and in him meant merely that he exchanged an act for a dream. He was filled with a supreme pity, even for the Devil, whom he called "that immortal scapegoat of gods and men."

He died on an evening of July, while the scent of hay in passing waggons filled and pleased his nostrils, lying in his half-monastic, half-manorial home, not far from Oxford. How often had he celebrated the sweetness of the dead grass as an emblem of comely human death ! For a little while he spoke of his friends, of the " beautiful gate " of St. Mary's, of his columbines (the older sort), and of a copy of Virgil newly come from Italy. We listened silently. Life was still an eloquent poet on his lips. But Death was a strong sculptor already at work upon his face and hands. The last waggon passed below his window as he lay dead, and the friendly carter shouted " Good-night."

Now, we three were ashamed that we could find no tears for the loss of such a man ; and again, that we should suffer any alteration of our joy, at having seen what we had seen. We recalled the past through half the night. As we sat, none of us looked more alive than he, amidst the old gloomy furniture, refashioned by the moon. We were but the toys of night, of the smooth perfumes and the sounds of nothing known, and of the presence which was like a great thought in the room. Then as the coming day mingled with the passing night, a cold pale beam—ὦ φάος ἁγνὸν—came to the four. As often a symbol becomes an image, so the beam of light seemed to be the very spirit of which it was a messenger, hailed by our eyes and hearts. It was beautiful as the Grail with many angels about it,—awful as the woman of stern aspect and burning eyes that visited the dream of Boethius. It was worthy to have ushered visions yet more august. Ah ! the awful purity of the dawn. The light grew ; our fancies were unbuilt ; we became aware of a holy excellence in the light itself, and enjoyed an almost sensual melancholy repose. The owls were silent. The night-ingales joined their songs to the larks'. And I went out and walked and remembered his epitaph — *Vita dulcis, sed dulcior mors*—and another July day, when Philip Amberley was alive.

How he would walk! with what an air, an effluence, humble, and of consequence withal! Half the village dallied among their flowers or beehives to see him going. His long staff was held a foot from the upper end, which almost entered his beard. He bore it, not airily with twirling and fantastic motion, as our younger generation likes to do, but solemnly, making it work, and leaning on it as if it were a sceptre, a pillar, a younger brother. His eyes appeared to study the ground; yet indeed all that was to be seen and much that is commonly invisible lay within their sway. It was said he kept eyes in his pockets. His shanks were of the extreme tenuity that seems no more capable of weariness than of being diminished. Returning or setting forth, especially when seen against the sky at sunset or dawn, he was a portent rather than a man. His person was an emblem of human warfaring on earth—a hiero-glyph—a monument. His movements were of epic significance. His beard did not merely wag; it trans-acted great matters. In setting out he himself said he never contemplated return; it was unnecessary; at most it was one of several possibilities. Yet had he a big laugh that came from his beard like a bell from a grey tower. He would even sing as he walked, and was the sole appreciator of his own rendering of "The All Souls' Mallard," in a broken, grim baritone.

All day we walked along an ancient Oxfordshire road. It was the most roundabout and kindly way towards our end, and so disguised our purpose that we forgot it. The road curved not merely as a highway does. Demurring, nicely distinguishing between good and better, rashly advancing straight, coyly meandering, it had fallen in love with its own foibles, and its progress was not to be measured by miles. At one loop (where the four arms of a battered signpost all pointed to—nowhere) the first man who trod this way must have paused to think, or not to think, and have lost all aim save perambulation. So it stole through the land without arresting the domesticities of the quiet hills. Often it was not shut out from the fields by hedge or fence or bank. For some leagues it became a footpath—its second childhood—"as though a rose should shut and be a bud again"—with grass and flowers unavoidable under foot and floating briers and hops overhead. In places the hedges had united and unmade the road. From every part of it some church could be seen : Philip would sometimes enter in, having some faith in the efficacy of reverence offered by stealth on these uncanonical holy days. On our way he sometimes paused, where bees made a wise hum in glowing gardens ; or where the corn-shocks looked like groups of women covered by their yellow hair, as the sun ascended ; or where the eye slumbered, and yet not senselessly or in vain, amidst a rich undistinguished landscape, made unreal and remote by mist; and he would whisper an oath or a line of Theocritus or a self-tormenting speech—"Six hundred years ago perhaps one of my name passed along this road. Oh! for one hour of his joy as he spied his inn, or carved a cross in the church of St. John, or kissed the milkmaid at yonder gateway. Or would that I could taste his grief, even; his fresh and lively grief, I think, had something in it which my pale soul is sick for. For me the present is made of the future and the past. But he—perhaps—he could say, 'Here am I with a can of mead and a fatigue that will do honour to my lavendered sheets; *Ave Maria!* here's to you all!'" Yet Philip's mood was not seldom as clear and simple as that.

At the inn—a classic inn to Oxford scholars—while the wind was purring in a yew tree, he put all his gloomier fancies in a tankard, where they were transmuted by a lambent ale and the "flaming ramparts" of that small world. The landlord was unloading a dray. As it is with men and clothes, remarked Philip, so with ale; the one grace of new ale is that it will one day be old. "May I," he said, "in some world or another, be at least as old as this tankard, in the course of time: if I deserve it, as old as this inn: if I can, as old as these hills, with their whiskers of yew. Or, so long as I am not solitary, may I be as old as the sun, which alone of all visible things has obviously reached a fine old age!" He told me that his only valued dream was of an immemorial man, seated on a star near the zenith; and his beard's point swept the hilltops, while with one hand he raised a goblet as large as the dome of the Radcliffe to his lips, and with the other stroked his beard and caused golden coins to flow in cascades into the countless hands of those underneath; and in a melodious bass he said continually, "It is well."

In his youth he had wedded Poverty, and when in the course of nature she forsook him, he gently transferred his heart to Humility, regretting only that he could no longer dress badly or make his own toast, without affectation. He would give a beggar a handful of tobacco, and ask sincerely, "Is it enough?" At the inn, he might have been lightly treated for the respect with which he shamed the most unhappy outcast, if he had not indifferently accepted the homage of the squire.

"Which book of the _Æneid_," said that magnate of fifteen stone, at seeing a Virgil in his hand, "do you like best?"

"The sixth."

"And why?"

"Because I have just read it over again."

"And which do you like next?"

"The second, because I read it first, and loved it (I was twelve) better than anything but rackets."

So he turned to the five tramps, the first I ever saw leave their hats undoffed at his approach, who sat opposite.

They spoke, proclaiming themselves human; but

their clothes, their twisted bodies, and their gnarled, grey, bare feet, seemed to be the original material from which some power had adventured to carve their desperate faces, and then desisted in alarm, lest it should make a gnome. They might seem to have newly risen out of the soil, with all its lugubrious dishonours about them, and in an elder world might have commanded the reverence of simple men, as Chthonian apparitions. I have seen dead pollard-willows like them, and rocks out of which the sea has wrought figures more humane. " Pedestalled haply in a palace court," they would have amazed the curious and confounded the wise ; drinking beer at " The Pilgrim's Chair," they happened to agree with Philip's "idea of a wild man," which he had treasured on a dusty Platonic shelf of his mind for fifty years. The *urpflanze* found at last could not bring a finer joy to a botanist than they to him. His mind wandered about his discovery. " These great men "—he said—" are the victims of a community that permits nobody to break its own law, and is indignant that a poacher or a thief should claim the foregone privilege. On these men falls the duty of keeping up the capacity of our race for breaking law—a natural capacity. I should like to see—fill the pot, landlord—something like the American arbor-day established in this fine country. On that day men should plant, not a tree, but a wild emotion. Not all of us, alas ! could find one to plant. But such a wild man's day would be a noble opportunity for the divine instincts that are now relieved or ill-fed by politics, fiction, religious reform, and so on. I am for a more than Stuart, indulgent, anti-parliament government on one day, when the policeman should clink tankards with the tramp, as if he too were a man. See here!"—he mildly concluded, exposing the unwilling palm of the nearest tramp,—" this good fellow is so appreciative that he has taken my coppers and left the silver in my purse." Ordering the landlord to fill tankards all round—" for this gentleman," he said, pointing to the pickpocket—he soon made the whole party harmonious, eloquent, and gay.

He spoke few words. His Virgil lay open still. Now and then his random speech or a laugh at a bad jest floated joyously—like lemons in a punch-bowl—over the company. Every one astonished every one with shrewd or witty things. Not a man but thought himself almost as fine a fellow as Philip Amberley. Not a man but on leaving him was a little abashed as he took a last glance at my friend, and saw what manner of man he was.

"There he goes," said Philip solemnly, as he leaned forward to watch them reeling up the lane, singing as if their feet were shod and their pockets full, "There he goes—an almost perfect man. I seem to see them as one man, made up of the virtues or unselfish vices (which are all the most of us can achieve) of all five, as a painter collects a beautiful face from many mediocrities. Every one of them has his fustian soul 'trimmed with curious lace.'" And so he continued; with generous and cunning speech freeing of rust, nay!

burnishing, the unused virtue in these abjects. " I have avoided what is called vice," he said, " because it is so easy, and I do not love easy things ; " and for the same reason he frowned but tenderly on those who had not avoided it.

While the sunlight was failing, we were left by ourselves. But Philip was not alone. He had laid his book and ale aside, and looked at the solemn row of empty chairs against the wall. His eyes wore the creative look of eyes that apprehend more than is visible. In those chairs he beheld seated what he called his Loves—the very faces and hair and hands of his dead friends. I have heard him say that they appeared "in their old coats." Night after night they revisited him—"of terrible aspect," yet sweet and desirable. They were as saints are to men whose religion is of another name than his. He could say and act nothing which those faces approved not, or which those faint hands would have stayed. Embroidered by the day upon the border of the night, their life was an hour. Out of doors he saw them, too, in well-loved places— gateways above Hinksey, hilltops at Cumnor or Dorchester, Christ Church groves, or fitting Oxford streets —such as (he believed) had something in them which they owed to his passionate contemplation in their midst. There he heard them speak softlier than the wings of fritillaries in Bagley Wood. *Si quis amat novit quid hæc vox clamat.* . . . But his own face comes not to satisfy the longing of those who watch as faithfully, with eyes dimmer or of less felicity.

Oxford

The Past

The Oxford graduate of the past is far too pale a
ghost in literature. He lies in old books, like a broken
sculpture waiting to be reconstructed, and survives but
in an anecdote and from his importance after leaving
Oxford for a bishopric or a civil place. For one
memory of a Don there are a hundred of soldiers,
statesmen, priests, in the quadrangles and streets. He
is in danger of being treated as merely the writer of a
quaint page among the records of the college muniment-
room. Erasmus, Fuller, Wood, Tom Warton, preserve and partly reveal the spirit of the past, and help
us to call up something of the lusty, vivid life which
the fellows and canons and presidents led in their
"days of nature." There is, for example, a Dean of
Christ Church, afterwards Bishop of Oxford and last
of Norwich, who has still the breath of life in him, on
John Aubrey's page.

I

He was "very facetious and a good fellow," and
Ben Jonson's friend. When a Master of Arts, if not
a Bachelor of Divinity, he was often merry at a good
ale parlour in Friar Bacon's study, that welcomed
Pepys and stood till 1779. It was rumoured that the
building would fall if a more learned man than Bacon
entered, a mischance of which the Dean had no fear.
When he was a Doctor of Divinity " he sang ballads at
the Cross at Abingdon on a market-day." The usual

94

ballad-singer could not compete with such a rival, and complained that he sold no ballads. Whereat "the jolly Doctor put off his gown and put on the ballad-singer's leathern jacket, and being a handsome man, and had a rare full voice," he had a great audience and a great sale of sheets. His conversation was "extreme pleasant." He and Dr. Stubbinge, a corpulent Canon of Christ Church, were riding in a dirty lane, when the coach was overturned. "Dr. Stubbinge," said the Dean, "was up to his elbows in mud, but I was up to the elbows in Stubbinge." He was a verse-maker, of considerable reputation, of some wit and abundant mirth, with a quaint looking backward upon old places and old times that is almost pathetic in these verses :—

> Farewell rewards and fairies,
> Good housewives now may say,
> For now foul sluts in dairies
> Do fare as well as they.
> And though they sweep their hearths no less
> Than maids were wont to do,
> Yet who of late for cleanliness
> Finds sixpence in her shoe ?
>
> Lament, lament, old abbeys,
> The fairies' lost command ;
> They did but change priests' babies,
> But some have changed your land ;
> And all your children sprung from thence
> Are now grown Puritans ;
> Who live as changelings ever since,
> For love of your domains.

When Bishop of Oxford, he had "an admirable, grave, and venerable aspect." But his pontifical state permitted some humanities, and he was married to a pretty wife. "One time," says Aubrey, "as he was confirming, the country people pressing in to see the ceremony, said he, 'Bear off there, or I'll confirm you with my staff.' Another time, being about to lay his hand on the head of a man very bald, he turns to his chaplain (Lushington) and said, 'Some dust, Lushington' (to keep his hand from slipping)." He and Dr. Lushington, of Pembroke College, "a very learned and ingenious man," would sometimes lock themselves in the wine-cellar. Then he laid down first his episcopal hat, with, "There lies the doctor"; next, his gown, with, "There lies the bishop'; and then 'twas "Here's to thee, Corbet" and "Here's to thee, Lushington." Three years after attaining the bishopric of Norwich he died. "Good-night, Lushington," were his last words.

II

There is also in Aubrey another such ruddy memory of a fine old gentleman—a scholar, a thoughtful and genial governor of youth, "a right Church of England man," and President of Trinity. In gown and surplice and hood "he had a terrible gigantic aspect, with his sharp grey eyes" and snowy hair. He had a rich, digressive mind, "like a hasty pudding, where there was memory, judgment, and fancy all stirred together," not suited to his day; and began a sermon happily, but not at all to Aubrey's taste :—

"Being my turn to preach in this place, I went into

my study to prepare myself for my sermon, and I took down a book that had blue strings, and looked in it, and 'twas sweet Saint Bernard. I chanced to read such a part of it, on such a subject, which has made me to choose this text. . . ."

He concluded, says Aubrey :—

"'But now I see it is time for me to shut up my book, for I see the doctors' men come in wiping of their beards from the ale-house.' He could from the pulpit plainly see them, and 'twas their custom in sermon to go there, and about the end of sermon to return to wait on their masters."

Undergraduates who pleased him not were warned that he might "bring an hour-glass two hours long" into the hall. He was inexorable towards wearers of long hair, and would cut it off with "the knife that chips the bread on the buttery hatch." It was his fashion to peep through key-holes in order to find out idlers. Says one : "He scolded the best in Latin of any one that ever he knew." It seemed to him good discipline to keep at a high standard the beer of Trinity, because he observed that "the houses that had the smallest beer had most drunkards, for it forced them to go into the town to comfort their stomachs." Yet in his exhortations to a temperate life, he admitted that the men of his college "ate good commons and drank good double beer, and that will get out." And he was a man of tender and exquisite charity. When he saw that a diligent scholar was also poor, "he would many times put money in at his window," and gave work in transcription to servitors who wrote a good hand. His right foot dragged somewhat upon the ground, so that "he gave warning (like the rattlesnake) of his coming," and an imitative wag of the college "would go so like him that sometimes he would make the whole chapel rise up, imagining he had been entering in." The Civil War, thinks Aubrey, killed the old man, just before he would have been fifty years President. For it "much grieved him that was wont to be so absolute in the college to be affronted and disrespected by rude soldiers." The cavaliers and their ladies invaded the college grove to the sound of lute or theorbo. Some of the gaudy women even came, "half dressed, like angels," to morning chapel. A foot-soldier broke the President's hour-glass. So he gathered his old russet cloth gown about him and closed his eyes upon the calamity and died, still a fresh and handsome old man.

III

John Earle, a notable scholar and divine of the seventeenth century, a fellow of Merton, and afterwards Bishop of Worcester and Bishop of Salisbury, has drawn the picture of "a downright scholar," which I may not omit. Earle had the most concentrated style of any man of his time ; each of his sentences is a document. His characters are as clear and firm as the brasses on Merton altar platform, and likely to endure as long.

"A downright scholar," he writes, "is one that has

much learning in the ore, unwrought and untried, which time and experience fashions and refines. He is good metal in the inside, though rough and unscoured without, and therefore hated of the courtier that is quite contrary. The time has got the vein of making him ridiculous, and men laugh at him by tradition, and no unlucky absurdity but is put upon his profession, and done like a scholar. But his fault is only this, that his mind is somewhat much taken up with his mind, and his thoughts not laden with any carriage besides. He has not put on the quaint garb of the age, which is now become a man's total. He has not humbled his meditations to the industry of compliment, nor afflicted his brain in an elaborate leg. His body is not set upon nice pins, to be turning and flexible for every motion, but his scrape is homely, and his nod worse. He cannot kiss his hand and cry Madam, nor talk idly enough to bear her company. His smacking of a gentlewoman is somewhat too savoury, and he mistakes her nose for her lip. A very woodcock would puzzle him in carving, and he wants the logic of a capon. He has not the glib faculty of gliding over a tale, but his words come squeamishly out of his mouth, and the laughter commonly before the jest. He names this word College too often, and his discourse beats too much on the University. The perplexity of mannerliness will not let him feed, and he is sharp set at an argument when he should cut his meat. He is discarded for a gamester at all games but 'one and thirty,' and at tables he reaches not beyond doublets. His fingers are not long and drawn out to handle a fiddle, but his fist is clenched with the habit of disputing. He ascends a horse somewhat sinisterly, though not on the left side, and they both go jogging in grief together. He is exceedingly censured by the Inns of Court men for that heinous vice being out of fashion. He cannot speak to a dog in his own dialect, and understands Greek better than the language of a falconer. He has been used to a dark room, and dark clothes, and his eyes dazzle at a satin doublet. The hermitage of his study makes him somewhat uncouth in the world, and men make him worse by staring on him. Thus he is silly and ridiculous, and it continues with him for some quarter of a year, out of the University. But practise him a little in men, and brush him over with good company, and he shall outbalance those glisterers as much as a solid substance does a feather, or gold gold lace." One story is told of him. He was sharp-tempered and much beloved ; his servitor was endeared to his faults, and inquired respectfully one day why his master had not boxed his ears. To which he replied " that he thought he had done so ; but indeed he had forgot many things that day " ; it being the day of Charles I.'s execution. Whereat the servitor wept, and received the admonition unexpectedly for his pains.

UNDERGRADUATES OF THE
PRESENT AND THE PAST

upon the road. The liberty of a man and the license
of a child are his together. Of course, he abuses them.
He uses them, too. Hence the admirable independence
of the undergraduate, which has drawn upon him the
excommunication of those whose concern is with the
colour and cut of clothes. He is the only true
Bohemian, because he cannot help it—does not try to
be—and does not know it. He is the true Democrat,
and condescension is far less common than servility
in his domain. He alone keeps quite inviolate the
principle of freedom of speech. It is indeed true that,
as anywhere else, fools are exclusive as regards clever
men and different kinds of fools ; and snobs, as regards
all but themselves. But theirs is a rare and lonely life.
At Christ Church they have actually a pool, in the
centre of their great quadrangle, for the baptism of
those who have not learned these fine traditions ; it is
appropriately called after Mercury, to whom men used
to sacrifice pigs, and especially lambs and young goats.
And there is no college in Oxford where any but
the incompatible are kept apart, and few where that
distinction is really preserved. As befits a prince in
his own palace, the undergraduate usually dispenses
with hypocrisy and secrecy, and thus gives an opportunity to the imaginative stranger. Such an one drew
a lurid picture of a horde of wealthy bacchanals, making
night hideous with the tormenting of a poor scholar.
It was not said whether the sufferer was in the habit of
doing nasty and dishonourable things, or had funked
at football, or worn ringlets over his collar : it was

almost certainly one of the remarkable efforts of imagination which are frequently devoted to that famous city and its inhabitants. The patience of the undergraduate is extreme. It is extended to tradesmen and to the sounds of the Salvation Army. He greets bimetallists with tenderness, teetotallers with awe, and vegetarians with a kind of rapture, tempered by a rare spurt of scientific inquiry. If he makes an exception against sentimentalism, he relents in favour of that place, "so late their happy seat," when he goes down. Mr. Belloc has put that retrospection classically :—

> The wealth of youth, we spent it well
> And decently, as very few can.
> And is it lost ?   I cannot tell,
> And what is more, I doubt if you can. . . .
>
> They say that in the unchanging place,
> Where all we loved is always dear,
> We meet our morning face to face,
> And find at last our twentieth year. . . .
>
> They say (and I am glad they say)
> It is so ; and it may be so :
> It may be just the other way ;
> I cannot tell.   But this I know :
>
> From quiet homes and first beginning,
> Out to the undiscovered ends,
> There's nothing worth the wear of winning,
> But laughter and the love of friends.
>
> .   .   .   .
>
> But something dwindles, oh ! my peers,
> And something cheats the heart and passes,
> And Tom that meant to shake the years
> Has come to merely rattling glasses.

Oxford

And He, the Father of the Flock,
Is keeping Burmesans in order,
An exile on a lonely rock,
That overlooks the Chinese border.

And one (myself I mean—no less),
Ah ! will Posterity believe it—
Not only don't deserve success,
But hasn't managed to achieve it.

Not even this peculiar town
Has ever fixed a friendship firmer,
But—one is married, one's gone down,
And one's a Don, and one's in Burmah.

   .   .

And oh ! the days, the days, the days,
When all the four were off together ;
The infinite deep of summer haze,
The roaring boast of autumn weather !

  .   .   .   .

I will not try the reach again,
I will not set my sail alone,
To moor a boat bereft of men
At Yarnton's tiny docks of stone.

But I will sit beside the fire,
And put my hands before my eyes,
And trace, to fill my heart's desire,
The last of all our Odysseys.

The quiet evening kept the tryst :
Beneath an open sky we rode,
And mingled with a wandering mist
Along the perfect Evenlode. . . .

I

The average man seldom gets into a book, though
he often writes one.   Yet who would not like to paint
him or have him painted, for once and for ever !   And,
a fortiori, who would not wish the same for the average

Undergraduates of the Present and Past

undergraduate ? I can but hint at his glories, as in an architect's elevation. For he is neither rich nor poor, neither tall nor short, neither of aristocratic birth nor ignobly bred. Briefly, Providence has shielded him from the pain and madness of extremes. He plays football, cricket, rackets, hockey, golf, tennis, croquet, whist, poker, bridge. In neither will he excel ; yet in some one he will for an hour be conspicuous, if only at a garden-party or on a village green. He never rashly ventures in the matter of dress, and when his friends who are above the average are wearing very green tweeds, he will be just green enough to be passable, and yet so subdued as not to be questioned by those who stick to grey. He is never punctual ; on the other hand, he is never very late. In conversation, he will avoid eloquence for fear of long-windedness, and silence for fear of appearing original or rude : at most, he will be frivolous to the extent of remarking, about a pretty face, 'Oh, she is *alpha plus* !' As a freshman only will he make any great mistakes. Thus, he will have several meerschaums ; will assemble at a wine party the most incompatible men, and conclude it by all but losing his self-respect ; and will for a term use Oxford slang as if it were a chosen tongue, and learn a few witticisms at the expense of shopkeepers, if he is free by the accident of birth. But he will speedily forget these things and become a person with blunt and tender consideration for others, and may be popular because of his excellent cigarettes or his ready listening. He will in a few years learn to row honestly, if not brilliantly; to know what is fitting to be said and read in the matter of books; to discuss the theatre, the government, the cricket season, in an inoffensive way. Add to this pale vision the colouring implied by a college hat-band and a decent, ruddy face, and you have the not too vigorous or listless, manly man, with modest bearing and fearless voice, who plays his part so well in life, and now and then—on a punt, or at a wedding—reveals to the discerning observer his university. The late Grant Allen knew him by his broad, brown back, and his habit of bathing in winter in a rough sea.

II

He has come to Oxford, much as a man of old would have come to some fabled island, out beyond the pillars of Hercules; for even so Oxford is out beyond the world which he knows—

> The Graces and the rosy-bosomed Hours
> Thither all their bounties bring.

Perhaps his schoolmasters have been Oxford men. But that has not disillusioned him. He has been in the habit of thinking of them as men who, for some fault or misfortune, have come back from the fortunate islands, discontented or empty. They have not known how to use the place: he knows, or will learn to know; and he dreams of it in his peaceful country school, or at a London school, where boys go as to a place of business, and make verses as others cast accounts. To

some Oxford men, Matthew Arnold's "Thyrsis" is
the finest poem that was ever written; and he knows
it by heart already; has sighed ignorantly over it;
and as his train draws near to Oxford, he repeats it to
himself, with a most fantastic fervour, as if it were
half a prayer and half a love-song, and certainly more
than half his own. The pleasant excited uncertainty, as
to whether he has seen the Fyfield elm, or whether that
oaken slope was Cumnor, and his happy surmises while
his eye skips from tower to tower in the distance, blind
him to the drizzling, holiday air of the platform: he
has no time to remember how it differs from East-
bourne: he is so set upon beholding the High Street
that he is indifferent to the tram and the mean streets,
and is not reminded of Wandsworth. The cabman is
to him a supernal, Olympian cabman. He pays the
man heavily, and quotes from Sophocles as he steps
through the lodge gate, amid the greetings of porter,
messenger, and a scout or two. The magnificent
quadrangle gives a dignity to his walk that is laughable
to senior men. He goes from room to room, making
his choice, and knows not whether to be attracted by
the spaciousness of one suite, or the miniature sufficiency
of another,—the wainscot of a third, the traditions of a
fourth, or the view from a fifth.

In the evening, at dinner in the college hall, he
puts all of his emotion into the grace before meat, and
by his slow, loving utterance robs the fellows of their
chairs and the undergraduates of their talk. He scans
curiously the healthy or clever or human faces of his

shut. But he returns quite cheerfully to his room, to read Virgil while the dreamy sky is still tender with the parting touch of night.

After breakfast, and some disbursements to porter and scout, he begins to make acquaintances, over a newspaper in the junior common room, or at a preliminary visit to his tutor. With one, he walks up and down High Street : he learns which are the tailors and which are not. With another, he goes out to Parson's Pleasure, and likes the willows of Mesopotamia, and sees New College Tower : he wants to loiter in the churchyard of Holy Cross, but is scornfully reminded that Byron did much the same. Queen's College inspires his companion with the remark that Queen's in Oxford is called "Quagger." The Martyr's Memorial calls forth "Maggers Memugger"; Worcester, "Wuggins"; Jesus, "Jaggers": and he is much derided when he supposes that the scouts use these terms.

After luncheon, he cannot get free, but must watch football or the humours of "tubbing" on the river. His companions, with all the easy omniscience of public-school boys, are so busy telling him what's what, that he learns little of what is. And at tea, he is as wise as they, and has the tired emotion of one who has been through fairyland on a motor car.

A week in this style broadens his horizon ; his optimism, still strong, embraces mankind and excludes most men. A series of teas with senior men and a crowd of contemporaries fails to exhilarate him. The

shy are silent : the rest talk about their schools ;
appear advanced men of the world ; and shock their
seniors, who in their turn dispense tales about dons,
and useful information : and he feels ashamed to be
silent and contemptuous of what is said. His grace in
hall has become so portentous that his neighbour hums
the Dead March in *Saul* by way of accompaniment.

With some misgiving he goes alone to his room,
sports his oak—which others so often do for him when
he is out—and puts his room in order. His college
shield, brilliantly and incorrectly blazoned, hangs above
the door. Photographs of his newest acquaintances
rest for the time upon his desk. He has not yet
learned to respect the photograph of a Botticelli above
the mantelpiece, and has tucked under its frame a
caricature of some college worthy, with visiting-cards,
notes of invitation, a table of work, and his first *menu*.
On the mantelpiece are photographs that recall tenderer
things, along with his meerschaum and straight-grained
briar. For a minute he is interrupted by a kick, an
undeniable shout, a cigar, and behind it the captain of
Rugby football.

"Can you play ? " says the captain.

"I have never tried," says the freshman, modestly.

The captain retires, after conferring an indignity in
pert monosyllables, and familiarly inquiring after "all
your aunts."

"How do you know I have any aunts, Mr. ——? "
he inquires.

"Oh," replies the captain, "I never heard of a

nephew without an aunt, and I am sure you couldn't do without several."

"I wonder why he came to Oxford," reflects the freshman.

"He's mistaken his calling," chuckles the other on the way downstairs.

The freshman lights his meerschaum (holding it in a silk handkerchief), and begins to make a plan for three or four years. But he never completes it. He believes Oxford to be as a fine sculptor, and wishes to put himself in its hands in such a way as to be best shapen by the experience, in a "wise passiveness." He wants to be a scholar, and fears to be a pedant. He wants to learn a wise and graceful habit with his fellow-men, and fears to be what he hears called a gentleman. He wants to test his enthusiasm and prejudices, and fears to be a Philistine. He wants to taste pleasure delicately, and fears to be a *viveur* or an æsthete. None of these aims is altogether conscious or precise ; yet it is some such combination that he sees before him, faint and possible, at the end of three or four years. Nor has he any aim beyond that. He will work, but at what? Neither has he realised that he will be alone and unhelped.

At first the loneliness is a great, and even at times a delirious, pleasure ; and whether he is in a church, or in the fields, or among books, it is almost sensual, and never critical. Oxford is, as it were, doing his living for him. He is as powerless to influence the passage of his days as to plan the architecture of his

dreams. He only awakens at his meals with contemporaries, and sometimes at interviews with tutors.
The former find him dull and superior. The latter
tell him that in his work he is indeed gathering honey,
but filling no combs; and find him ungainly and
vague. He consoles himself with the reflection that
he is not becoming a pedant or a careless liver. He
writes verses to celebrate the melodious days he lives.
All influences of men fall idly upon him—

> They on us were rolled
> But kept us not awake.

The digressive habit of mind not only grows upon
him; he cultivates it. His tutor says that it is
impossible to give a title to his best essays. Long,
lonely evenings with books only encourage the habit.
But he can defend it, and laughs at criticism.
Shakespeare's dramas, he says, flow through the
centuries, like the Nile; his flood is not so vast, that
it may not be aggrandised by many a tributary. It
has come down to us vaster than when it reached
Milton or Gray, not only by definite commentary,
but by the shy emotions of a myriad readers. We
add to it, he says triumphantly, by our digressions; and
what revelation it may make in consequence, to a far
future generation, we cannot guess. In his pursuit of
words, which soon enthrall him, he goes far, rather
than deep. Wherever the word has been cherished for
its own sake, in all " decadent " literature, he makes his
mind a home. He begins to write, but in a style

which, along with his ornate penmanship, would occupy a lifetime, and result in one *brochure* or half a dozen sonnets. It is a kind of higher philately. But it takes him to strange and fascinating byways in literature. He loves the grotesque. Now and then, he lets fall a quotation or even a dissertation on such a book at dinner, and suddenly he is launched into popularity.

First he is hailed as a decadent, and shrinks. When the shrinking is over, he secretly falls in love with the half-contemptuous title, and seeks others who accept it. Now he is never by himself. Those with whom he has no sympathies like him because he happens to know *Pantagruel* and a few books such as some undergraduates keep between false covers. His room is fragrant with unseasonable flowers, with the perfume of burning juniper, burning cassia, and cedar, and sweet oils. What if the honourable ghosts of Oxford frown upon his strange devotions? He is at least living a life that could not persist elsewhere. At chapel, he is reading Theophrastus. He is studying an undercurrent of the Italian Renaissance at a lecture on Thucydides. As if he were to live for ever, and in Oxford, his existence is such that his stay in Oxford or in life becomes precarious. He is reputed to be a connoisseur in wines, pictures, and sixteenth-century furniture. He is a Roman Catholic by profession, an agnostic by conviction; yet no religion or superstition is quite safe from his patronage. He mistakes the recrudescence of childishness for a sad and wise maturity. Freshmen are struck by his listless gaiety and the unkind and seeming wise solemnity of his light expressions. If to sit sumptuous and still, to discourse melodiously of everything or nothing, to be courteous, sentimental, cold, and rude in turns, were wisdom, he is wise. He acquires the lofty cynicism of the under-informed and the over-fed. He can talk with ease and point, about the merely married don, about virtue as the fine which the timid pay to the bold, about the dulness of enthusiasm and the strange beauty of grey. At what is temperate and modest he throws satire with a bitterness enhanced by a secret affection for what he lapidates. Like a man who should paint an angel and call it a thief, he narrowly pursues his own choicest veiled gifts with a malicious word. In short, his brilliant conversation proves how much easier it is to think what one says than to say what one thinks. Yet is he now a harder student than he has ever been, and allows nothing to disturb him at his books. He has nodded at European literatures through half their courses, in the lonely hours when his companions are asleep. He is planning again, and realises that it would be a showy thing to get a first class. His conversation becomes gloomy as well as bitter. People suspect that he means what he says; and he mutters in explanation that experience is the basis of life and the ruin of philosophies. His friends simply accept the remark as untrue. He is now often reduced to silence among those who sleep well. He no longer pours a current of fresh and illuminating thought upon things which he not only does not understand, but does not care for, in politics or art.

He slips out of brilliant company, to enter occasionally among religious circles where they are tolerant of lost sheep, and has begun to pay his smaller bills and to find out what books he must read for a degree, when the examination day arrives. Then he borrows his old dignified look of indolence in the sultry schools, while he writes hard, and secures a second class by means of a legible handwriting, clear style, and amusing irrelevance. He goes down, alone, still with a fascinating tongue, desperate, and yet careless of success, ready to do anything so long as he can escape comfortable and conventional persons, and quite unable to be anything conspicuous, but a man who has been to the garden of the Hesperides and brought back apples that he alone can make appear to be golden in his rare moments of health.

III

He is one who knows that three or four years at the University is a good investment. He comes up with an open scorn of idlers, both gilded and gifted. Whether he is clever and successful or not, he has a suspicion that dons are underworked, colleges expensive hotels or worse, and is determined to change all that. Not infrequently such a one is perverted by a happy evening with a few acquaintances, early in his first term. If he is not, he is a white elephant. The dons are alarmed by his instructions, the undergraduates by his clothes. "If this were not an old conservative creek," he seems to say, "promotion would go by merit, and I should

117

soon be at the top of the tree and begin repairs." But the University remains unchanged.

He looks about him for a more stealthy passage to his ends.

A vernal impulse, it may be, sends him to a tailor's shop, and in the unwonted resplendence that follows he is almost a butterfly. In a jocular spirit he calls upon the persons whose invitations he used to ignore. If he is clever or amusing, or apparently labouring under a delusion, he is liked. In his turn he is called upon. He begins to find that there is something in himself which has a taste for all that is human. *Homo sum*, he mutters, with one of the classical quotations which are to his taste. He will dally with the multitude for an hour or two,—a week,—why not for a term? When he is in the company of the sons of old or wealthy families, it occurs to him that rank and wealth are powerful : it follows, and can be demonstrated, that the power cannot be more justly exercised than in the furthering of honest and meritorious poverty. He will make a concession ; possibly another visit to a tailor ; perhaps a little champagne. Several discoveries follow.

It would be not only difficult, but contemptible, to play football or to row ; yet he can learn to play lawn tennis. He is presently quite at home, if not in love, at garden parties. He mistakes the curious interest of men and women, in one who is entirely different from themselves, for a compliment to his adaptability.

Society bores him rapidly. He has had enough of

vacation visits and picnics during the term, and revives his acquaintance with work and the indolent fellows. But that is not necessarily attractive. Also, his friends and admirers will not let him disappear ; and he returns to frivolity in a serious and plotting spirit. He tolerates nearly every one, and in particular the influential. They cultivate him, clearly, for his intelligence, his independence, his originality. Why should he not cultivate them for their own petty endowment ? He enters office at the Union. He is elected to presidentships, secretaryships.

He is lucky if he does not learn from others—what he will not easily learn alone—that his resemblance to them is neither his best nor his most useful quality. And so he finds that after all there is nothing in ideals, and steps into a comfortable place in life ; or perhaps he does not.

IV

The many-coloured undergraduate looks as if he had been designed by the architect of the " Five Orders Gate " in the Schools' Quadrangle. His hat, his face, his tie, his waistcoat, his boots, represent the five orders ; as in his great original, the Corinthian is predominant, and like that, he would never be thought possible, if he had not been seen. Yet he moves. Despite his elaborate appearance—destined to endure perhaps for all time, or as long as a shop-front—it is impossible to guess what may be his activities. He may be a famous oarsman or cricketer, in which case his taste forbids him to adopt the broad blue band of his rank, unless there are ladies in Oxford.   He may be a hard-working student who adopts this among many methods of showing that his successes fall to him as naturally as Saturday and Sunday.   He may be an amateur tragedian, or magazine-wit, or æsthete, who finds the costume less embarrassing although less distinguishing than cosmetics and an overcoat of fur.   He may be a billiard-player who has chosen this contrasted, barry, wavy set of colours as his coat of arms, or the perambulating *mannequin d'osier* of several tailors, a transcendental sandwich-man.   Or he may be a "blood" of many great connections and expenses ; genial in his sphere ; pleased with the number of his debts and the times he has been ploughed in " Smalls " ; hunting or rowing keenly, while he lasts ; and except when he has to work (which sends him to sleep), a sitter up at nights over cards and wine—

> Strict age and sour Severity,
> With their grave saws, in slumber lie.
> We that are of purer fire
> Imitate the starry quire.

Or his great expenses and connections may not exist. He is perhaps a poor and worthless imitation of all that is great,—who does not know Lord X., of whom he tells such dull stories, — whose relatives are neither retired, nor in Army, Navy, or Church,—and entirely respectable in the Vacations, when he earns by his own self-sacrifice what was earned for his models by the unscrupulousness of their ancestors. In short, he may be a most brilliant, most fascinating, or most modest person, who has chosen to appear piebald.

His room is decorated with photographs of actresses, along with perhaps a Hogarth print, a florid male and a floral female portrait, an expensive picture of a horse, and copies from Leighton. In a corner is a piano, which he is perhaps eager and unable to play. The air is scented with roses and cigarettes. The window-seat is strewn with hunting-crops, bills, a caricature of himself from an undergraduate paper, several novels and boxes of cigarettes, a history of the Argent-Bigpotts of Bigpott, and, under a cushion, some note-books and a table of work.

He is to be met with everywhere; for he is not ashamed to be seen. He lives long in the memories of travellers from Birmingham who wait five minutes in Oxford. In the Schools he is a constant attendant, always sanguine, not quite cheerful or satisfied with the company, yet equal (at his Viva Voce) to a look of ineffectual superiority for the man who ploughs him with a smile. He is also to be found by the river, during the Eights, when he cheers and looks very well; in a bookshop, where he recognises Omar and some novels; or in the High, which never wearies him, although his bored look seems to say so.

Oxford

V

He has come up with a scholarship from school.
There, he took prizes, had an attack of brain-fever,
and edited the magazine : and he has come to the
University as if it were an upper class of his old school.
His aim is, as many prizes as possible and a good
degree. The tutors here, like the masters at school,
he regards as men who turn a handle and work up
more or less good material into scholars, as a butcher
makes sausages, all exactly alike to the eye, out of a
mysterious heap. At first he is in great awe of a
fellow, and wears his scholar's gown at its utmost
length, and as proudly as star and riband—he will
hardly take it off in the severe quarter of an hour in
which he permits himself to drink coffee and eat
anchovy toast after dinner ; and he sometimes pretends
to forget that he has it on until he goes to bed.
Perhaps on one occasion he trips his tutor over a
quotation or something of no account. He scans the
tutor's bookshelves, and finds odd things between
Tacitus and Thucydides which make him ponder. At
length, he is less respectful ; opens discussions, in
which, having tired the tutor, he returns very well
satisfied. For he has a patent memory, as he has a
patent reading-lamp and reading-desk. Nothing goes
into it without a bright label, as nothing goes into his
note-book without honours of pencilled red and blue.
His copy of Homer is so overscored that one might

suppose that the battle of the pigmies and cranes had been fought to a sanguinary end upon its page.

At school his football was treated with contempt, yet with silence, except by very small boys. At college he is anxious to do a little at games. The captain of the boats asks him, as a matter of course, to go down to the river, to be tubbed (or coached) in a pair-oar boat ; and he replies that he "will willingly spare half an hour." He shows some good points at the river ; is painstaking and neat. His half-hour is mercilessly multiplied day after day. He is to be found at the starting-point in February, in his college Torpid, and proves a stately nonentity or passenger ; discovers that rowing abrades more than his skin, and gives it up just before he is asked to. For the future he sculls alone, once a week, when it is mild, and oftener when his friends are visiting him—which he does not encourage. At such times he learns that it is quite true that Oxford possesses some fine drawings, marbles, stained glass, and a library of little use to a determined "Greats" man. These he exhibits to the visitors impatiently and with pride. He returns to his work unruffled. Already he has scored one First Class and a *proxime* for a prize. Yet his tutor pays him qualified compliments, which he attributes to the natural bitterness of a second class man. The tutor sometimes asks him what he reads ; to which he replies brightly with a long list of texts, etc.

"Yes, but what do you read when you unbend?" says the tutor. "Did you ever read *Midshipman Easy?*" (with a touch of exasperation).

Oxford

The youth blushingly replies: "No, I never unbend."

Nor is the other far more pleased when he brings with him, on a short vacation boating holiday, a volume of the *Encyclopædia Britannica*.

Now and then he speaks at the Union. There and at afternoon teas with ladies he is known for the lucidity of his commonplaces and the length of his quotations. For the most part he talks only of his work and the current number of the *Times*. His work, meantime, is less and less satisfactory to every one but his coach. Some say that he will get another first, and will not deserve it. Already he is learning that three or four years among "boys" is not helpful to his future. No one so much as he emphasises the distinction between third and second year undergraduates. He is always looking for really improving conversation, and play of mind without any play. A book tea would please him, if it were not so frivolous.

Once only he lapses from the rigidity of his ways. He thinks it a matter of duty until it occurs, when the hearty and informal reception given to his rendering of "To Anthea" discourages any further condescension. With that exception, he moves with considerable dignity among mankind: in all things discreet, with a leaning towards the absurd; in most things well under control, yet, in spite of his rigidity, really luxuriating in the sweets of a neutral nature that never tempts temptation. He sends in a neat, flowery, and icy poem for the Newdigate Prize, and wins. He gets his second First

Class and an appointment which he likes at the same
time. He enters for a fellowship, and his failure calls
forth the old story about the cherry tart that was
offered to likely competitors at a fellowship examination, where the cleanest management of the stones
meant success.

He goes down with his degree, and confident,
applauded, unmissed. His friends say that he lacks
something which he ought to have. What is it?

VI

He has come up to Oxford with an unconquerable
love of men and books and games; is resolved not to
be careful in small matters for a few years; and has a
clear vision of a profession ahead. Others think that
a fellowship and a prize are his due; he vaguely regards
them as nice. But he has a strong belief that any kind
of distinction is dangerous at Oxford, and among the
least of its possibilities. He respects the scholar and
the Blue, and sees that they might equally well be made
in another city or on another stream. Bent upon a
life among men, he sees that a university is a place
where many are men, but where many of the suspicious
and calculating passions of a bigger world are in abey-
ance; and thinks that it should therefore be the home
of perfect rivalries and friendships.

He will attend the lectures of ———, which are outside his course. He will accept some hearty excesses
in the rooms of ——— as equally important. When he

comes up his sympathies are universal. He is eager and warm in his liking of men and things ; and he is straightway on happy terms with undergraduates and dons. After a few terms his versatility is hard-worked in order to give something more than an appearance of sympathy in the company of athletes, reading men, contemplative men, and wealthy men. For a time his success is sublime. The reading man thinks there was never such a student. The rowing man approves of his leg-work and his narratives at those little training parties for the enjoyment of music, port, and fruit— "togger ports." His method appeals to the don. Now and then, indeed, some one a little more reticent than himself puts him to a test, and he may discourse on Aquinas to a Unitarian Socialist, or on Gargantua to one deep in Christian mysticism or fresh from the new year's advice of his great-aunt. In such cases, either he is repulsed with sufficient narrowness on the part of the other to supply a necessary balm, or he makes a surprised and admiring convert, who may do odd things on account of his inferior versatility. For quite a long time he may have the good fortune to let loose his interest in the Ptolemies in the neighbourhood of other admirers or neutral gentlemen. And so long all is more than well. He is popular, exuberant, and in a fair way of growth, albeit a little overdone. It is true that in tired moments he is likely to choose the path of least resistance and find himself in not very versatile company. But what a life he leads ! what afternoons on the Cherwell between Marston and Islip in the summer ; and beyond Fyfield, when autumn still has all that is a perfecting of summer in its gift! The admiring plodder who hears his speeches says that he will some day be Lord Chancellor. His verses have something beyond cleverness in them : they have a high impulsion, as when spring makes a crown imperial or a tulip. And listening to his talk or reading his letters, one might think that he will be content to be one of those men of genius who avoid fame—but if their letters are unearthed two hundred years hence they will have the life of Wotton's or T. E. Brown's. His friends think that such a clear-souled, gracious, brilliant creature would leaven the Senior Common Room and draw out the shyness of ——, and twist the neck of ——'s exuberant dulness.

The liberal life, close in friendship with so many of the living and the historical, on occasions almost gives him the freedom of all time. His friends note that Catullus or Lucan or Dante is nearer to him than to other men. He quotes them as if he had lived with them and were their executor, and by his sympathy seems to have won a part authorship of their finest things. He expounds the law and makes it as exhilarating as the *Arabian Nights*, or as if it were a sequel to *Don Quixote*. And in history the dons notice his picturesqueness, which is as passionate as if he could have written that ardent sonnet :—

> The kings come riding back from the Crusade,
> The purple kings, and all their mounted men ;
> They fill the street with clamorous cavalcade ;
> The kings have broken down the Saracen.

Oxford

Singing a great song of the Eastern wars,
In crimson ships across the sea they came,
With crimson sails and diamonded dark oars,
That made the Mediterranean flash with flame.
And reading how, in that far month, the ranks
Formed on the edge of the desert, armoured all,
I wish to God that I had been with them
When the first Norman leapt upon the wall,
And Godfrey led the foremost of the Franks,
And young Lord Raymond stormed Jerusalem.

So the glories of youth and history and summer mingle in his brain and speech.

No one is so married to his surroundings as he, and while he appears to many to be shaped by them—beautiful or grotesque—as an animal in a shell; to a few he appears also to shape them, so that Oxford in his company is a new thing, as if it were the highest, last creation of the modern mind. He does not acquiesce in the limp mediævalism of the rest, but recreates the Middle Ages for himself, finding new humanities in the sculptures, and beauties in the perspective, strange sympathies between the monkish work and the voices and faces of those who sit amidst it. In his own college he effects a surprising " modernisation " by removing a little eighteenth-century work and revealing the fifteenth-century original. Thus all history is to him a vivid personal experience.

But he is overwhelmed by his versatility, and cultivates that for its own sake, and at last loses his sympathy with all who are not as he. The athletes begin to treat him as a poser. The hard workers stand aloof from his extravagances. With different sets he is treated and rejected as a man of the world, a hepatetic philosopher, a dilettante; . . . some speak of the literary taint; the dons are tired. He is in danger of becoming the hero of the most unstable freshman and his scout. And so, though he has perhaps but one failing more than his contemporaries, and certainly more virtues, he is ridiculed or feared or despised, and goes about like Leonolo in the play, who wandered

> Because perhaps among the crowd
> I shall find some to whom I may relate
> That story of the children and the meat—

until he has the good luck to fall back upon his friends. There he is safe again. His name will indeed be handed down through half a dozen undergraduate generations for his least characteristic adventures, but if that is a rare distinction, and equivalent to a press immortality, it is likely to be of no profit to him. Where he used to be an expensive copy of a Bohemian, he becomes at last as near the genuine thing as any critic, with a wholesome fear of being absolute, would care to pronounce. His one pose is that of the plain-spoken, natural man, in the presence of a snob. Everywhere he is as independent as a parrot or a tramp. In life, few are to be envied so much. For he achieves everything but success.

VII

The important undergraduate is one who has been thunderstruck by the inferiority of the rest. He can-

not, if he would, be rid of the notion. In a large
college the distinction between himself and others is
cheerfully acknowledged by them, while he leads a
painful life. In a small college, for a year or two, he
is so handled that he may sometimes wish he were as
other men are. At the end of that time he has by
contagion created a covey of important men, and now,
to his moral, athletic, and intellectual excellence, and
his superior school, is added the excellence of being
several years older than the majority. He establishes
a despotism for the good of the college. He is willing
to take the fellows into partnership, makes advances,
and, when coyly repulsed, has his sense of importance
increased by the knowledge that an opposition exists.
His splendour is marred only by the stranger, who
mistakes his brass-buttoned blazer for a livery, and
finds his pomposity well worthy of such fine old
quadrangles,—and requests him with a smile and half
a sovereign to exhibit the chapel and the hall, and "tell
me who are the swells"!

He walks about Oxford with a beautiful satisfaction.
"A poor thing, but my own," he seems to say, as he
enters the college gate. Little boys in the street pull
off their caps as he passes, and the saucy, imprudent
freshman does the same. He rows, he plays football
and cricket, he debates, all indifferently, but with such
an air that he and even some others for a time believe
that he is the life and soul of the college.

He has been captain and president of everything,
when he finds that there is no further honour open to

him, and he muses almost with melancholy. The others find it out somewhat later ; he is dejected. Though fallen, he is still majestic. He stalks about like a foxhound in July, or like a rebellious archangel—

Is this the region, this the soil, the clime? . . .

Once more October returns. A new generation of freshmen is invited to tea, and for one glorious hour his old vivacity returns, as he questions, instructs, exhorts. "The President of the O.U.B.C. once said to me, . . ." or "When I was in the college boat and we made seven bumps . . ."—such are his conjuring terms.

Perhaps in a few years he returns, to find that the college is not what it was, and that his nickname is still remembered.

VIII

He is one whom the Important Undergraduate regards as a parody of himself. For he resembles the other in no respect. He is a clean, brave, and modest freshman, with too great a liking for the same qualities in others to be disturbed by any faulty affectations that may go along with them. When he comes up he has a few friends in Oxford, keeps them, and is well contented. He plays his games heartily, and is almost as glad to cheer, when he is not good enough or pushing enough to play. Nothing can destroy his regular habits, and at first he narrowly escapes being despised for them by his inferiors. He is comparatively poor and not very clever.

Oxford

Neither has he any amusing oddities, or stories to tell, or much whisky to dispense. Yet he finds notoriety thrust upon him. If it were not for his firm and blushing manner, he would never have his room empty for work. Very soon, he is the only man in the college who may sport his oak with no fear from the thunders of distant and idle acquaintances. Every one wishes to possess him. The athletes cannot withstand his running, his hard fielding. The more unpopular reading-men are first attracted by his simple habits as a freshman, and then surprised that they are not repulsed when they hear that he will get his Blue ; he is always their protector. The elegant and stupid men, at least for a few terms, know no man who so becomes a cigar, and is so fit to meet their female cousins at breakfast. The brilliant men like him first because he is a mystery ; next, because he recalls to them their "lost youth," which was nothing like his ; and finally, because he is so friendly and so naïvely rebukes their most venturesome sallies. His presence in a room is more than a wood fire and a steaming bowl. He seems to know not sorrow—

Clear as the sky, withouten blame or blot.

It is sorrow-killing to see his amazement at sorrow, like the amazement of those spirits in Purgatory who exclaimed, as Dante passed : "The light seems not to shine on one side of him, though he behaves as one that lives." Men of very different persuasions are fascinated by "the young Greek" in the Parks or on the river. He is successful everywhere, and is in time captain of football and president of the debating and literary society, although his knowledge of literature is confined to Scott's Novels, *Hypatia*, and the *Idylls of the King*. He accepts the advice of the Important Undergraduate, here and elsewhere, and unconsciously ignores it, with happy results. For his contemporaries believe that he has launched his college upon one of those sudden, mysterious ascensions that mean social, learned, and athletic improvement at once. To the last he is diffident, and at the same time always capable of doing his best. " Can you clear that brook ? " one asks in the Hinksey fields. " I don't know," is the reply, and over he goes, a foot clear amongst the orchis. Not a great deal more powerful than the cox, he strokes a boat that has never been bumped, and is the only oar whom the rest all praise. To see him halting over a commonplace speech at a college function, or making the most ludicrous new verses to the alphabetical song of " Jolly old Dons," and winning applause ; or dropping his head on his knees at the winning-post on the river ; or carried for the hundredth time round the quadrangle on some festive night—is, nobody knows or asks why, an inspiration. And after his last farewell dinner he smiles, as if he knew everything or had the *pitié suprême*, as he notices the follies which he supposes he is " not clever enough for," and goes down to his manor or country curacy very happily.

Oxford

IX

There was for a short time, amidst but not of the University, a student whom I cannot but count as a "clerk of Oxenford." He came from no school, but straight from a counting-house. All his life he had been a deep, unguided delver in the past. An orphan in the world, he had chosen his family among the noble persons of antiquity. Cæsar was more real to him than Napoleon, and Cato more influential than any millionaire. He had tasted all the types, from Diogenes to Seneca and Lucullus. When he tired of his counting-house, he tried to imagine a resemblance between it and a city state, but was himself but a helot in the end.

So it happened that he came to live in a cottage attic, five or six miles from Oxford. He wanted to be a university man. He despised scholarships as if they had been the badge of the Legion of Honour. Colleges he would have nothing to do with, because they spoiled the simplicity of the idea of a university in his mind. They had made possible the social folly of Oxford. But in his reading of history he had travelled no farther than the Middle Ages towards his own time; and a picture of Oxford life in that day fascinated him. He believed that it was still possible to lead the unstable, independent, penniless life of a scholar; and he knew not why a student should hope or wish to be anything like a merchant or a prince. A merchant had money, and a prince flattery : he would have wisdom. It was likely to be a long search, and in his view it was the search that was beyond price. He wanted wisdom as a man might want a star, because it was a rare and beautiful thing. So his studies were a spiritual experience. The short passages of Homer which he knew by heart had something of religious unction in his utterance.

He left London afoot, with a parcel of books strapped to his shoulders; his only disappointment coming from a landlord who refused to pay for his singing with a meal, as he would have done six hundred years ago. A farmer treated him generously, under the belief that he was mad.

A few antiquated Greek texts and notes, an odd volume of Chronicles from the Rolls Series, and an Aldrich, adorned his room, and with their help he hoped to lay the foundations of a seraphic, universal wisdom. Gradually he would become worthy to use the Bodleian and contend with the learned gown and hostile town.

Once a week, in the beginning, he walked into Oxford. He saw the river covered with boats, and laughed happily and pitifully at men who seemed to know nothing about the uses of a university. A good-tempered youth, in rowing knickerbockers, was a fit disciple for his revelations, he thought, and was about to preach, when he barely escaped from a bicycle and a megaphone. Almost sad, murmuring Abelard's line

Sunt multi fratres sed in illis rarus amicus—

135

he hastened to the city. The spires gave him courage again, and he ran, singing an old song :—

> When that I was a scholar bold,
> And in my head was wealth untold :
> Heigh ! Ho ! in the days of old
> In Oxford town a scholar trolled.

Every one in a master's gown received a bow. He was mistaken for a literary man. And once in Oxford, he went, seriously and as if at a ceremony, through a minutely prepared plan. He attended service at one of the churches, and especially St. Mary's. He took long, repeated walks up and down High Street, and into all the lanes, which he hardly knew when their names had been changed. Then he sat for an hour in the oldest-looking inn. In blessed mood, he tried the landlord unsuccessfully with Latin, and waited until some scholar should call and exchange jests with him in the learned tongue, or perhaps join him in a quarrel with the town. The only scholar that called talked in a strange tongue, chiefly to a bull-pup, and never to him. And late at night he stole reluctantly home, never so much pleased as when, in a dark alley, he was saluted by a proctor, and asked if he might be a member of the University. But the little note inviting him to be at —— College at —— A.M. on the following day never came, and he was cheated of the glory of being the first member of the University who could by no means pay a fine.

At the end of this holy day he spent the night with his books, thinking it shame to sleep away the ardent, memoried hours that followed. When sleep caught him at last, with what happiness and pomp he walked down St. Aldate's and along Blue Boar Street and Merton Street, and came suddenly upon Wren's domed gate at Queen's! or paused in St. Mary's porches, or found the inmost green sanctuary of Wadham Gardens!

Once he dreamed that on a Sunday he preached from the little outdoor pulpit at Magdalen, where he mounted by some artifice of sleep's. The chamber windows and quadrangles were full. His voice rose and linked to him the crowd outside in High Street. All remained silent, even when it was known that the hieroglyphics were skipping from their perches in the cloister and carrying off large numbers, no one knew whither. Those that were spared—and his voice rose ever higher, and expanded like the column and fans of masonry at Christ Church—were stripped of their waistcoats and ties and all their luxuries and dignities. Their hair was shaved : presently they were all cowled, and with a great shout hailed him Chancellor. He floated down from the pulpit and led them down the High, evicting the pampered tradespeople and fettering all parasites. Singing a charging hymn, they marched in procession to St. Mary's, and thence to a feast at Christ Church hall ; when he awoke with the din of revelry.

Sometimes, in his dreams, he saw enacted the Greek tragedies, to the accompaniment of the organs of New College and the Cathedral.

Now that he knew his plays by heart, he came oftener

to Oxford, and gained the freedom of the Bodleian. Every day he came, bringing his own books to fill the interval before the library books arrived, although for the most part he stared at the gilt inscriptions outside his alcove window, or at the trees and roofs farther off. When he was hidden among the expected volumes he read but feverishly. He put questions to himself in the style of the schoolmen, and pondered "whether the music of the spheres be verse or prose." He tingled all over with the learned air, and was intoxicated by the dust of a little-used book. The brown spray that fell from a volume on the shelf before him was sweeter than the south wind. Week after week obscured his aims. The only moments of his old chanting joy came to him in his still undiluted expectations, when he came in sight of the city—

O fortunati quorum jam mœnia surgunt !—

and at night, while the river shone like an infinite train let fall from the shoulders of the city.

He sold his books in Little Clarendon Street, and whenever he wished to read, there he found them and others ready. Most of his time passed in the corner of an inn, where he sat at a hole in the dark window as at a hagioscope, and with heavy eyelids watched the University men. And it was possible to earn a living by selling the *Star* for a penny, night after night, and to have the felicity of dying in Oxford.

Undergraduates of the Present and Past

THE PAST

I

Whilome ther was dwellynge at Oxenford
A riche gnof, that gestès heeld to bord,
And of his craft he was a carpenter.
With hym ther was dwellynge a poure scoler,
Hadde lernèd art, but al his fantasye
Was turnèd for to lern astrologye,
And koude a certeyn of conclusions,
To demen by interrogaciouns,
If that men sholde have droghte or ellès shoures.
Or if men askèd him what sholde bifalle
Of everythyng, I may nat rekene hem alle.
    This clerk was clepéd hendè Nicholas.
Of deernè love he koude, and of solas,
And ther-to he was sleigh and full privee,
And lyk a mayden mekè for to see.
A chambrè hadde he in that hostelrye
Allone withouten any compaignye,
And fetisly y-dight, with herbès swoote,
And he himself as sweete as is the roote
Of lycorys, or any cetèwale.
His Almageste, and bookès grete and small,
His astrelabie, longynge for his art,
His augrym stonès, layen faire apart,
On shelvès couchèd at his beddès heed.
His presse y-covered with a faldyng reed,
And all above there lay a gay sautrie,
On which he made a-nyghtès melodie
So swetèly, that al the chambrè rong,
And *Angelus ad Virginem*, he song ;
And after that he song the "Kyngès noote" ;
Ful often blessèd was his myrie throte,
And thus this sweetè clerk his tymè spente
After his freendès fyndyng and his rente.

Such was a "clerk of Oxenford" in Chaucer's day,
living probably on the generosity of a patron, and
differing only from his patron's son, inasmuch as he

was saved the expense of a fur hood. In the rooms of most, Bibles, Missals, or an Aristotle or Boethius, took the place of the Almagest of the astrologer ; and more conspicuous were the rosaries, lutes, bows and arrows of the undergraduates. In their boisterous parti-coloured life of almost liberty, even an examination was a vivid thing, and meant a disputation against all comers in a public school, to be followed by a feast of celebration, visits to taverns, and probably a dance,

After the scole of Oxenfordè tho ;

and so, after a fight with saucy tradesmen or foreigners, to bed, or Binsey for a hare, or to other night work.

II

"A meere young Gentleman of the Universitie is one that comes there to weare a gowne, and to say hereafter, he has been at the Universitie. His Father sent him thither, because hee heard there were the best Fencing and Dancing Schools. From these he has his Education, from his Tutor the oversight. The first element of his knowledge is to be shewne the Colleges, and initiated in a Taverne by the way, which hereafter hee will learne for himselfe. The two marks of his Senioritie, is the bare velvet of his gowne, and his proficiencie at Tennis, where when he can once play a Set, he is a Freshman no more. His Studie has commonly handsome shelves, his Bookes neate silk strings, which he shows to his Father's man, and is loth to untye or take downe for feare of misplacing. Upon foule days for recreation hee retyres thither, and looks over the prety booke his Tutor reades to him, which is commonly some short Historie, or a piece of *Euphormio*; for which his Tutor gives him Money to spend next day.   His maine loytering is at the Library, where hee studies Armes and bookes of Honour, and turnes a Gentleman Critick in Pedigrees.   Of all things hee endures not to be mistaken for a Scholler, and hates a black suit though it be of Satin.   His companion is ordinarily some stale fellow, that has been notorious for an Ingle to gold hatbands, whom hee admires at first, afterward scornes.   If hee have spirit or wit, he may light of better company, and may learne some flashes of wit, which may doe him Knight's service in the Country hereafter.   But he is now gone to the Inns of Court, where he studies to forget what hee learn'd before, his acquaintance and the fashion."

From the *Microcosmographie*.

III

The younger Richard Graves (1715-1804), a contemporary of Shenstone and Whitfield at Pembroke, has sketched, in his own person, the unstable undergraduate of sixteen, in his progress from set to set.   It is a very lasting type.   "Having brought with me," he writes, "the character of a tolerably good Grecian, I was invited to a very sober little party, who amused themselves in the evening with reading Greek and drinking water.   Here I continued six months, and

141

we read over Theophrastus, Epictetus, Phalaris' *Epistles*, and such other Greek authors as are seldom read at school. But I was at length seduced from this mortified symposium to a very different party, a set of jolly, sprightly young fellows, most of them west-country lads, who drank ale, smoked tobacco, punned, and sang bacchanalian catches the whole evening. I began to think them the only wise men. Some gentlemen commoners, however, who considered the above-mentioned very low company (chiefly on account of the liquor they drank), good-naturedly invited me to their party ; they treated me with port wine and arrack punch ; and now and then, when they had drunk so much as hardly to distinguish wine from water, they would conclude with a bottle or two of claret. They kept late hours, drank their favourite toasts on their knees, and in short were what were then called 'bucks of the first head.' "

IV

The Lownger

I rise about nine, get to Breakfast by ten,
Blow a Tune on my Flute, or perhaps make a Pen ;
Read a Play till eleven, or cock my lac'd Hat ;
Then step to my Neighbour's, till Dinner to chat.
Dinner over, to *Tom's* or to *James's* I go,
The News of the Town so impatient to know :
While *Law*, *Locke* and *Newton*, and all the rum Race
That talk of their Modes, their Ellipses, and Space,
The Seat of the Soul, and new Systems on high,
In Holes, as abstruse as their Mysteries lye.
From the Coffee-house then I to Tennis away,
And at five I post back to my College to pray :

Undergraduates of the Present and Past

> I sup before eight, and secure from all Duns,
> Undauntedly march to the *Mitre*, or *Tuns*;
> Where in Punch or good Claret my Sorrows I drown,
> And toss off a Bowl to the best in the Town:
> At one in the Morning, I call what's to pay,
> Then Home to my College I stagger away.
> Thus I tope all the Night, as I trifle all Day.
>
> From the *Oxford Sausage*.

V

I have taken from Glanvil's *Vanity of Dogmatizing* the original version of the story of Matthew Arnold's Scholar Gypsy.

"There was very lately a lad in the University of Oxford, who being of very pregnant and ready parts, and yet wanting the encouragement of preferment, was by his poverty forc'd to leave his studies there, and to cast himself upon the wide world for a livelyhood. Now, his necessities growing dayly on him, and wanting the help of friends to relieve him, he was at last forced to join himself to a company of Vagabond Gypsies, whom occasionally he met with, and to follow their Trade for a maintenance. Among these extravagant people, by the insinuating subtilty of his carriage, he quickly got so much of their love and esteem; as that they discovered to him their Mystery: in the practice of which, by the pregnancy of his wit and parts he soon grew so good and proficient, as to be able to outdo his Instructors. After he had been a pretty while well exercised in the Trade; there chanc'd to ride by a couple of Scholars who had formerly bin of his acquaint-

143

ance. The Scholars had quickly spyed out their old friend among the Gypsies ; and their amazement to see him among such society, had well nigh discovered him ; but by a sign he prevented their owning him before that crew, and taking one of them aside privately, desired him with a friend to go to an Inn, not far distant thence, promising there to come to them. They accordingly went thither, and he follows: after their first salutations, his friends enquire how he came to lead so odd a life as that was, and to joyn himself with such a cheating, beggarly company. The Scholar Gypsy having given them an account of the necessity, which drove him to that kind of life ; told them, that the people he went with were not such Imposters as they were taken for, but that they had a traditional kind of learning among them, and could do wonders by the power of Imagination, and that himself had learnt much of their Art, and improved it further than themselves could. And to evince the truth of what he told them, he said he'd remove into another room, leaving them to discourse together ; and upon his return tell them the sum of what they had talked of. Which accordingly he performed, giving them a full account of what had pass'd between them in his absence. The Scholars being amazed at so unexpected a discovery, earnestly desired him to unriddle the mystery. In which he gave them satisfaction, by telling them, that what he did was by the power of Imagination, his Phancy binding theirs ; and that himself had dictated to them the discourse, they held together, while he was from them : That there were warrantable wayes of heightening the Imagination to that pitch, as to bind another's ; and that when he had compass'd the whole secret, some parts of which he said he was yet ignorant of, he intended to leave their company, and give the world an account of what he had learned."

COLLEGE SERVANTS
OF THE PRESENT AND THE PAST

CHAPTER V

The Present

The fact that no porter or other college servant has recently received a D.C.L. is no proof of his insignificance. "The President and your humble servant manage very well between us," said one porter, with perfect truth. College servants are the corbels and gargoyles that complete the picturesqueness and usefulness of Oxford. The oldest are not so much serviceable as quaint, often grotesque, reminders of an age that has gone ; their faces are apt to express grim judgments upon the changes which they have helplessly watched ; and they are among the stoutest retainers of the past. The younger are either very much like any other good men-servants, silent, receptive, curious but uninquiring, expensive, and better able to instruct than to learn ; or they are average men, with Oxford variations. In spite of their profound knowledge of the richer classes, they remain, as a body, good conservatives, with the half-sarcastic, half-reverent servility of their order. They do not often change; the men whom they serve are replaced every year by others; and looking on at generation after generation, they are not only skilled and practical psychologists, and almost the only persons in Oxford who wear silk hats on Sunday, but perhaps the most enduring human element in the University. "Well," says an eighteenth-century "scout" to another to-day, in an undergraduate "dialogue of the dead" —"Well, I suppose gentlemen are no worse and servants no better than in my time?" "Such a thing is impossible" was the reply. Yet one may surmise that they are more plutocratic, at least, than they were, if it be true that every summer at a Scottish hotel one may find "Mr. and Mrs. Brown of —— College, Oxford" on the pages of the visitors' book, in a handwriting known to the buttery. In the game which they play with the undergraduates, they know all their opponents' cards. Yet, until a member of the University is admitted to the cellar and pantry parliament, they will always be praised as reticent and discreet. A little inexperience will soon reveal, as the freshman knows, the other qualities of the college servant.

I

He awakens you every morning by playing with your bath, and is a perpetually recurring background to the sweet disquiet of your last half-hour in bed. In serving you, he serves himself; and late in the day he

is to be seen with a wallet on his back, bent under such
" learning's crumbs " as half-empty wine-bottles and
jars of Cooper's marmalade. In these matters he has a
neat running hand, without flourishes. No man has the
air of being so much as he the right hand of fate.
When he drinks your wine and disappoints a joyous
company, when he assumes your best cigars, and leaves
only those which were provided for the freshman of
taste—so inevitable are his ways that you can only hope
sarcastically that he liked the fare. He appears to have
a noble scorn of cash, when he asks for it ; and you are
bound to imitate. All the wisdom of the wise is cheap
compared with his manner of beginning a speech with,
" If you please, sir, it is usual for freshmen to, . . ."
while he is dusting your photographs. He is blessed
with an incapacity to blush. His politics are those of
the majority ; his religion has something in common
with that of all men. He could be conscientiously
recommended for a post in a temple niche or a street
corner, with the inscription " For twenty years a mate
at sea, and blinded in the pursuit of my duties," or
" Crippled in childhood." He is equalled only by his
" boy," who is perhaps older than himself. I remember
one such. I should like to have known his tailor, who
must have had a genius for style, for fitting aptest
clothes for men. His coat was as many-pocketed as
Panurge's, and as wonderful. Its bulges and creases
were an epitome of —— ; its " hang " might serve as
the one true epitaph, if suspended over his tomb. With
all his faults, he had that toleration which the vicious

often extend to the good, but do not often receive in return. He was a fellow of infinite wiles that were wasted but not thrown away in a world of three or four quadrangles and a buttery. Full of traditions, he was their master, not their prey ; and though he was the shadow of great names, he seemed conscious of being their inheritor too. For he had served men who had got fellowships and even Rugby or rowing Blues. With leading cases out of this mighty past he defended his misdemeanours and supported his proposals. In vain he toiled after time ; he was always a generation behind. If a man failed in "Smalls" or Divinity, he was told that Mr. ——, the "Varsity three-quarter," did no less, and Mr. ——, who rowed at Henley and was sent down after a bonfire, was ploughed four times. "Lightly like a flower" he wore his honours, tyrannising over men who never got Blues and were never sent down, and smiling away awe and ridicule alike. "I never saw nor shall see such men as Pirithous, . . ." he might have said ; it mattered little to him ; and even Pirithous was only respected after many years, when he had become an investment of the "boy's." He quoted wise saws, was full of advice, offered with a kind of humility and yet indifference, because you were so small a factor in his self-satisfaction.

> High on your summit, Wisdom's mimick'd Air
> Sits thron'd, with Pedantry her solemn sire.
>
> In every glance and motion you display,
> Sage Ignorance her gloom scholastic throws
> And stamps o'er all your visage, once so gay,
> Unmeaning Gravity's serene repose.

College Servants of the Present and Past

And so he goes through life, with all the pomp of learning—of the reality, none—complacent, imposing, and yet hardly a man.

II

Of the college cook it is easy to say too much. He is a potentate against whom there is no appeal on earth. "Much knavery," says Ben Jonson, "may be vented in a pudding." In the days of the *Shotover Papers* he could offer in exchange for a recipe "an introduction to some country families." At the monastic door of his kitchen, as he meditates his mysteries, something of the Middle Ages clings to him yet, and he is half an abbot, contemptuous of a generation that makes small demand upon his subtlety and wealth. It is said that he comes of brilliant ancestry and has fallen. What heights there may be in the world from which a man could be said to fall in becoming a college cook, I do not know. For years he made clear the distinction between fancy and imagination. By fancy he lived, and on his fancies generations fed. He could disguise the meanest materials, and make them illustrious, subtle, or exquisitely sweet. He was *animal propter convivia natum*. In his grey kitchen, with chestnut beams aloft, a visitor seemed to assist at the inauguration of a perpetual spring. On the one hand was the earth—the raw material—the mere flesh or fish ; and out of this, with upturned sleeves, like artist or conjuror, he made the flowers flourish and the leaves abound. By the perfume, it was a mysterious indoor Mayday. And so

153

he lived, and was feared and respected. But it was admitted that he had rivals. Something in a grander style was yet to be done. . . .

It was mid-February. Wherever I looked, I saw first the cold white sky above and the snow beneath, and secondly the red faces of skaters out of doors, and indoors the blaze of great fires and the purple and gold of wine. Winter was to be met in every street—white-haired, it is true, but nevertheless a lusty, red-faced fellow, redder than autumn, with a grip of the hands and a roaring voice. As I passed the kitchen, the cook was silently at work. His hair was like the snow, his face like the fire. The brass, steel, pewter, and silver shone. The kitchen, with its fragrance, lustre, and quietness, was like an altar. There, too, was the priest, with stainless vestment and sacerdotal bearing. And as I left him and mounted the stairs, I seemed unblest. I found Scott tedious, Pater excessive, and Sir Thomas Browne a trifler, and threw them aside. Soon there was a knock at the door, and a man—a throne, domination, princedom, virtue, power—swept magnificently in. A light and a warmth, beyond the power of fire to bestow, accompanied him. He bent down solemnly and laid a little white covered plate upon the hearth. Before I could speak — "the gods themselves are hard to recognise"—he was gone. I uncovered the plate with something of my visitant's solemnity—

> Fair spirit of ethereal birth,
> In whom such mysteries and beauties blend !
> Still from thine ancient dwelling-place descend,
> And idealise our too material earth ;

> Still to the Bard thy chaste conceptions lend,
> To him thine early purity renew ;
> Round every image, grace majestic throw ;
> Till rapturously the living song shall glow
> With inspiration as thy being true,
> And Poesy's creations, decked by thee,
> Shall wake the tuneful thrill of sensuous ecstasy.

It was the climacteric of his career, and he shall go down to posterity upon the palates of men, not as one who worked out his recipes to three places of decimals, or as a distinguished maker of " bishop " or " posset," or as one worth his weight in oysters, but as the creator of that necessary which is in fact brown bread, toasted and buttered.

III

Most pontifical of all college servants was old Acamas, who was not long ago to be seen, in his retirement, apparently beating the city bounds, and now and then standing sentry and defender of some old gate or archway. I first noticed him in the chapel quadrangle of ——, and could almost have mistaken him for a fellow of the old school, such was his aspect, and the reverent, half-wondering air with which he surveyed the buildings. But he took off his hat to the junior fellow, and I was undeceived. There was something pathetic in that salute. He was himself apparently far worthier than the young man in flannels of the chapel and the ancient arms ; and he seemed to know it, as he bent and trembled over his stick to declaim :—

" He may be a very clever young gentleman, but,

bless me, it is not the Greek that makes the scholar.
There was the old President, who never looked at his
book, and was all for horses ;—but he had a way with
him ; he would swear just so, so ; he was a scholar, if
ever a man was. But the new ones are just all book or
all play. They came in about the same time as bicycles
and steam ploughs and such nonsense. And there's too
much lady about the college now ; and such ladies !
they are so dressed that it is hard to tell which of them
is quite respectable. . . ."

And so he went on, a little less reverent than he
looked. But it was only a crimson heat of old age, and
soon passed.

What a fine, decent figure he was. He was clothed
in a dull black suit, with black tie, and an old-shaped
hat, and wore his gloves. He had unquestionably a
professional mien, and could not have been a gardener
or groom. He was something old, settled in the land
and known to the stars, traditional. His sorrow was
nothing less dignified than disestablishment. It was
time to be going. The enemy was in possession and
insulting. He had been in the Balliol fellows' garden
ages ago, and knew what a line the old buildings made
against the sky, and what the scene is now. He would
walk about, hoping to express a volley of scorn by his
silence to persons with no ear for silence. He never
went into Tom quad at Christ Church without missing
the figure of Mercury—perhaps a copy from John of
Bologna, and taken down early last century—which
used to preside over the fountain, still known as

College Servants of the Present and Past

"Mercury," and used as a water ordeal or court of ultimate appeal by undergraduates. "That old pagan fellow," he used to say, "told you more about the size of that quadrangle than the guide-books do"; and certainly nothing short of that or a playing fountain would so pleasantly expound the spaciousness of Wolsey's square. When some one proposed burning in effigy certain officials at the time of Edward VII.'s coronation, he "did not remember that such things were done at George's."

He stopped to look at the new buildings of the college, and pointing at the whitened stone, said, "I don't believe that stone is stone at all." As he passed an entry, full of bicycles, he said sadly, without a thought of scorn, "It was built by public subscription," and with his hand in his pocket, he seemed to be thinking that the finest thing in the world was to be the sole founder of a college. He once had a distant prospect of the Banbury Road, and would like to make night beautiful with its burning.

He still leaves Oxford by coach, or not at all. I believe that he calls Market Street "Cheyney Lane," and Brasenose Lane "St. Mildred's," and Pembroke Street "Pennyfarthing Street." To hear him talk of St. Scholastica's day gives one a pretty notion of the antiquity of Oxford and himself. In 1354, on that day, several scholars found fault with the wine of a city vintner, and threw it at his prosperous face. The vintner gathered his neighbours and threatened. St. Martin's bell was rung, and the city made fierce preparations at the accustomed summons. Then St. Mary's bell was rung, and the University came forth with bows and arrows and slings. "Slay," and "Havock," and "Give good knocks," cried the citizens. The fight was long and bloody, and disastrous to the scholars. So for many centuries the city had to appear penitentially at St. Mary's on St. Scholastica's day. In 1825 this institution ceased at the corporation's request. But Acamas will never forgive them, and hardly the University for giving way. "When laudable old customs dwindle, 'tis a sign learning dwindles," he would say, as Hearne said, when there were no longer any fritters at dinner. Nor is he to be moved by the mundane glories of his college in the schools or elsewhere. A brilliant "examinee" of the college, and his particular aversion, having gained a First in Law, when it was pointed out to him by the scholar's scout, the old man remarked : "And now I hope he knows what a privilege it is to belong to this college."

How slow and decorous he was at the buttery hatch, performing even his own business as if he were about that of another. He carried a plate as if it were a ceremony ; and his imperturbability would have completely endowed a railway porter and several judges. In hall, when once the needs of all the diners had been supplied, he would stand like " Teneriffe or Atlas unremoved," an effigy, a self-constituted symbol of olden piety and order, bent on asserting sweet ancient things, while fellows raced into hall, and undergraduates raced out. He was one with the coats of arms emblazoned on the panels or the glass, and the benefactors' portraits up among the shadows of the roof timber, and with the dial on the grass, which says, " I change and am the same."

He is now seldom outside the old city wall, unless he goes in May to the river through Christ Church or between Merton and Corpus. When he sees Tom tower he makes the melancholy revelation that he once heard Tom boom one time less than the appointed number. As for the flowers in the window-boxes, it is " cook's work " ; he has seen the like ornament " on pastry." On a bank holiday he is clothed in extraordinary dignity and gloom, and stands with an expression that wields a mace, in the hope of repelling the pleasure-seeker from some holy or learned retreat. If he were not mistaken for an eminent person, it would fare ill with those whose footsteps he dogs, lest they should commit some desecration. He can hardly permit smoking in the quadrangles, and has to turn his back to avoid seeing the accursed thing. At one time, a man dared not run through the purlieus of the Divinity School, for fear of the nod of Acamas.

He is a mirror of good manners, which he has learned out of love, and not necessity. He has a great store of antique information—statutes, precedents, fables—which, as in an aumbry, he keeps fragrant by much meditation, and is pleased to display. His elaborate courtesies are interpreted almost as insults by the new generations ; men wonder what they have done to deserve his withering respect. It is reported that on one occasion, at twilight, a vigorous gentleman brushed past him, between the Camera and Brasenose. Acamas turned, with a soft and bitter protest against "a gentleman forcing what he could command." "If," said he, "the Vice-Chancellor were here, he should know that a gentleman had insulted an old college servant by mistaking him for a townsman." . . . He bowed and almost broke his heart when he recognised the beaming face of the Vice-Chancellor.

He is the corrector of all new abuses and the defender of old, and through his father, a college butler and long since dead, he has the times of Trafalgar fresh in his mind, with imposing third-hand memories of the days when Oxford was Jacobite. The subtle distinguishing marks of all the colleges, as far as concerns fashions of morals and manners, scholarship and sport, he knows by heart, and professes such an experienced acquaintance with like matters that in the High or by the Long Bridges he knows at sight a "Greats" man or a "Stinks" man or a mathematician; of which last he is a determined hater; and when on one occasion he remarked on the good looks of a certain plain person, he was forced to explain that he meant "good-looking for a mathematician." He would at need devise a new coat of arms for Magdalen or St. John's, or improve "the devil that looks over Lincoln."

Of "his own college" he knows everything, from the cobweb on Jeremy Taylor in the library to the oldest beam in the kitchen roof. He knows the benefactors and their benefactions, their rank, and everything but the way to pronounce their names ; and has a kind of unofficial bidding prayer in celebration of their good deeds. His ideal of a head of a college is an odd mixture of Dean Gaisford and Tatham of Lincoln ; for he demands some eccentricity along with dignity and repute, and in the course of three-quarters of a century he has combined the two. The common-room chairs he knows better than those who sit in them —their history and their peculiarities, and who have sat therein. By nice observation he is aware of the correct way of crossing a quadrangle, and of whose furniture should be consumed in bonfires. The spires and gate-ways of the city are close friends to him, and " Isn't *she* beautiful," or " Isn't *he* looking well," or " They have their little ways," is his comment as he passes one or other of the things that have brooded over his life continually. He can tell when the bats will come out of the tower in a fine January or a windy March ; when the swifts shall scream first by All Saints'; and the colour of New College tower when a storm is due from the west. I can think of him as being the deity of the place, in a mythopœic age, and picture him *corniger*, with fritillaries in his hoary locks, as the genius of Isis, up in a niche at the Bodleian.

Oxford

The Past

I have no doubt that the past had many such to show, and that the present, when it has graduated into a past, will not be found wanting ; but the ways of the college servants of old are buried deep in oblivion. They were less numerous then, when a senior and a junior student slept in the same room, and the latter made the beds, etc. Upon scholars, Bible-clerks, and the like, fell a great many of the duties which are now the scout's—as waiting at the fellows' table in hall, and the pleasanter although more thankless task of calling up the fellows and more luxurious commoners in the morning. Not only was the scholar or "servitor" a practical servant for part of his time, but the regular servants could be students also, and we may guess from the Corpus statutes that they must sometimes have attended lectures and have taken degrees. A story runs that a vain scholar had sent some Latin verses to his tutor by the hand of a servant, who quickly read and corrected them, to the humiliation of the scholar, when he received them back, with the comment, that his work seemed to have been revised by one who was acquainted with the Latin tongue. No doubt a man of this stamp often rose, or if he stayed in college made his attainments profitable. A man who was once manciple at Wadham became a noted maker of mathematical instruments. The manciple bought and distributed provisions in the college : the cook or

College Servants of the Present and Past

cooks and butlers were sometimes called upon to furnish a banquet of " nine hundred messes of meat, with twelve hundred hogsheads of beer and four hundred and sixteen of wine," as at Balliol, when a Chancellor of twenty-two years of age was installed : the porter was prominent, but as yet much subordinated to the head of the college, to whom he delivered the keys at an early hour : the barber, who was sometimes also the porter, was the welcome dispenser of true and false news, and at Wadham survived until the sixties of last century, when he insisted that the amateur actors should have their wigs dressed by him, under pain of being betrayed to the Warden. Of the old servants— *heu prisca fides*—we can only guess at the devotion, from the story of old Thomas Allen's servitor, who was overawed by his master's mathematical instruments and his reputation of astrologer, and would " impose on freshmen or simple people " by telling them that spirits were often to be met coming up Allen's staircase " like bees." John Earle has preserved the ways of an old college butler, from his experience as a fellow of Merton.

" An old College Butler is none of the worst students in the house, for he keeps the set hours at his book more duly than any. His authority is great over men's good names, which he charges many times with shrewd aspersions, which they can hardly wipe off without payment. His Box and Counters prove him to be a man of reckoning ; yet he is stricter in his accounts than a usurer, and delivers not a farthing

163

without writing. He doubles the pain of *Gallobelgicus*, for his books go out once a quarter, and they are much in the same nature, brief notes and sums of affairs, and are out of request as soon. His comings in are like a Tailor's from the shreds of bread, the chippings, and remnants of the broken crust : excepting his vails from the barrel, which poor folks buy for their hogs, but drink themselves. He divides a halfpenny loaf with more subtility than *Kekerman*, and subdivides the *a primo ortum* so nicely, that a stomach of great capacity can hardly apprehend it. He is a very sober man, considering his manifold temptations of drink and strangers, and if he be overseen, 'tis within his own liberties, and no man ought to take exceptions. He is never so well pleas'd with his place, as when a Gentleman is beholding to him for showing him the Buttery, whom he greets with a cup of single beer and sliced manchet, and tells him 'tis the fashion of the College. He domineers over Freshmen when they first come to the Hatch, and puzzles them with strange language of Cues and Cees, and some broken Latin which he has learnt at his Bin. His faculty extraordinary is the warming of a pair of Cards, and telling out a dozen of Counters for Post and Pair, and no man is more methodical in these businesses. Thus he spends his age, till the tap of it is run out, and then a fresh one is set abroach."

THE OXFORD DAY

CHAPTER VI

THE OXFORD DAY

With cares that move, not agitate the heart.

IN other cities the past is a tradition, and is at most regretted. In Oxford it is an entailed inheritance. Nevertheless, by way of a gaudy foil to this hale immortality, fashions flourish there more luridly, and fade more suddenly, than elsewhere. Afraid, therefore, that I might stumble upon anachronisms unaided, I addressed myself as a seeker after truth to several freshmen who might have been expected to know practically everything. One wished to be excused because he was standing for the secretaryship of the Union, and was "somewhat out of touch with ordinary life." He had been busily opening debates in half the colleges of Oxford, in order to prove his sound principles and high capabilities, and enclosed this table of labours :—

11th inst., at —— : "That in the opinion of this house His Majesty's government has done its best."

12th, at —— : "That the struggles of the poor towards a larger and freer life are not to be discouraged."

13th, at —— : "That vegetarianism is opposed alike

167

to our traditions and our present needs." Also later
(to oppose) : " That a wave of imperialism causes a
reformation in the standards of literature."

(14th, twenty-first birthday.)

18th, at —— : " That poets are the interpreters of
their age."

19th, at —— : " That in encouraging sports this
University approaches more nearly to the Greek ideal
than at any other period of its existence has been the
case."

20th, at —— : " A paper on ' Mentality in Life and
Art.' "

21st, at —— : " That Oxford has not sufficiently
realised and reformed its national position since
imperialism became an acknowledged fact."

Another gentleman of more tender years and less
exuberance forwarded the *menu* of his college junior
gaudy, in itself a pleasant reminder of the more solid
occupations of undergraduates. He had made a table
of a day's life, alongside the dishes, like this :—

	Soup
Macedoine.	*The Senior Proctor.*
	Fish
Turbot and Lobster Sauce.	*My tailor : and to buy a meerschaum.*
	Entrées
Tomates Farcées.	*My Coach.*
	Joint
Saddle of Mutton.	*If possible, my philosophy tutor.*
	Game
Pheasants.	*Aristotle.*

168

The Oxford Day

He had " no time for more."

Of the third answer I can just see this fragment, in a fine confident penmanship, among the flames : " Oxford life falls under three heads, which I shall discuss separately. They are Religion, Education, and Social Life. And first of Education. My tutor breakfasts at eight. He has forty-eight pupils, and four ladies from Somerville College. He has one lecture and to-morrow's to prepare. In the afternoon he will be fresh and cheerful at the college barge, watching the races. He is writing two books, and is on the Board of Guardians. In spite of this the great thing about Oxford education is the way it stamps a man—'the cast of Vere de Vere,' as the poet says ; no matter in what position in life his lot is thrown, a certain easy grace——"

I find a more rational description of an Oxford day as it was in 1867, and as it was up to the publication of Mr. Rhodes's will, in the *Oxford Spectator*, one of the most enduring of undergraduate periodicals.

" The whole History of Philosophy," says the writer, E. N[olan], " is simply the story of an ordinary Oxford day. . . . In the morning, when I awake, the eastern dawn, as it shines into my room, gives my philosophy an Oriental tinge. I turn Buddhist, and lie thinking of nothing. Then I rise, and at once my tenets are those of the Ionics. I think, with Thales, that Water is the great first principle. Under this impression I take my bath. Then, yielding to Animaxander, I begin to believe in the unlimited, and straightway, in a rude toilette, consume an infinite amount of breakfast. This leads to the throwing open of my window, at which I sit, an unconscious disciple of Anaximenes, and a believer in the universal agency of Air. I lock my door and sit down to read mathematics, seeming a very Pythagorean in my loneliness and reverence for numbers. I am disturbed by a knock. I open the door and admit my parlour-maid, who wishes to remove the breakfast things. She is evidently an Eleatic, for she makes an abstraction of everything material, and reduces my table to a state of pure being. Again I am alone, and as I complete my toilet before my mirror, I hold, as Heraclitus did, the principle of the becoming, and think that it, and it only, should be the rule of existence. I saunter to the window, and ponder upon the advantages or otherwise of taking a walk. I am kept at home by some theory of the Elements, such as possessed Empedocles. Now I bethink me of my lunch, and I become an Atomist in my hunger, as I compare the two states of Fulness and Void. At last Atomistic Necessity prevails, and I ring my bell. Lunch over, I walk out, and am much amused, as usual, with the men I meet. I notice that those who have intellect superior to their fellows neglect their personal appearance.

The Oxford Day

These, I think, are followers of Anaxagoras : they believe in νοῦς, and they deny the Becoming. Others I noticed to be bent upon some violent exercise. I feel myself small and weak beside them, wondering much whether I, who to them am but half a man, am man enough to be considered, sophistically, the measure of all things. I console myself with remarking to myself that I surely know my work for the Schools better than they. Behold! I am Socratic. Virtue, I say, consists in knowing. So I chatter away to myself, feeling quite Platonic in my dialogue, until I meet a luckless friend who is to be examined next day in Moderations. I walk out with him far into the country, talking to him about his work, and struggling against my deeply-rooted antipathy to exertion of any kind. Surely Aristotle could not have been more peripatetic, or Chrysippus more Stoical. The dinner-hour makes me Epicurean, and I pass unconsciously over many stages of philosophy. I spend an hour in the rooms of a friend who is reading hard for honours. I come away but little impressed with the philosophy of the Schoolmen. The evening passes like a dream. I have vague thoughts of recurring to my former good habits of home correspondence ; but this revival of letters passes by, leaving me asleep in my chair. Here, again, as at dinner, I doubtless pass through many unconscious stages. At length I begin to muse upon bed. It is a habit of mine to yield to the vulgar fascinations of strong liquors before retiring for the night. Philosophy, I learn, works in a circle, ever returning unto itself. It is for this reason, perhaps, that my last waking act is inspired both by Hegel and Thales. Hegel prompts me to crave for Spirit : Thales influences me to temper it with Water."

Yet, if the Oxford day, as is fitting, can always be expressed in terms of philosophy, it is sometimes more complex, often more simple than that ; and it is longer. It begins and ends at 7 A.M. At that hour, the student and the fanatical novel-reader, forgetful of time, the passive Bacchanalian, and the man who prefers the divine, long-seated Oxford chair to bed, are usually persuaded to retire ; for unacademic voices of servant and starling begin to be heard in the quadrangle. The blackbird is awake in the shrubbery. Very soon the scout will appear, and will not know whether to say "Good-night" or "Good-morning," and with the vacant face of one who has slept through all the blessed hours of night, will drive men to bed. There is a dreamy laying aside of books—volumes of Daudet and Dickens, Fielding and Abbé Prévost, Morley, Roberts and Poe,— old plays and romances,—Stubbs, and the Chronicles, Stuart pamphlets,—Thucydides, Aristotle, and later Latin than Quintilian. If there is to be a Divinity examination later in the morning, there are Bibles scattered up and down, epitomes, and a sound of men's voices asking the difference between one and another version of a parable, and "Who was Gallio ?" and preparing all the playful acrobatics that will pass for knowledge in the Schools. While these are trying to sleep, with the gold sunlight winning through their eyelids, one or two picked men are rising of their own free will, and some because they have to run in the Parks before a training breakfast; others are arguing with themselves or with their scouts that it cannot possibly be nearly half-past seven; or later on, that a passing bell or a bell-wether has been mistaken for the college chapel bell; others expelling the awakening scout with more frankness: some doze and doze, with alternate pricks of conscience and necessity, and desperately deciding to rise, have to saunter about, too late for chapel, too early for breakfast; the majority murmuring that all is well, and enjoying the pleasantest of thefts from daylight; for, to the man who need not, or will not, rise, the chapel bell is a blithe and kindly spirit, that sets a crown upon the bliss of oncoming sleep and gives a keener edge to his complacency, as he thinks of the cold, sleepy virtue that walks in the world below. The chaplain, a man of habit, is also getting up. No one has ever seen a fellow late for chapel.

When the service is over, those who have attended are either awake or asleep again. The service itself is of an awakening kind, and has a vigour that is unknown outside Oxford.

> Oh, dear and saintly chaplain,
> Time toils after you in vain!
> When you stroked the Eight to glory,
> Did you prove this quite so plain,
> As at morning chapel daily
> And at evensong again?

Oxford

So run the verses which express the kind of vigour in vogue.

Now the perfervid reading man, and the man whose genealogical tree is conspicuous for a constant succession of maiden aunts, go to their cocoa and eggs : and, within three hours afterwards, the average man, to porridge, fish, eggs and bacon, coffee and oranges ; the decadent, to cigars, liqueurs and wafers ; the æsthete, to his seven wonders and a daffodil ; and some, of all classes, to the consolations of philosophy and soda-water. Only the last-named habitually break their fast in solitude.   For it is in Oxford the most social meal of the day.   It may begin at any time from eight until half-past eleven—anything later being "brunch"—and last until half-past one.   Some even believe that an invitation to breakfast embraces the afternoon.   Lectures seldom interfere with the meal, since the man who leaves for their sake is not usually missed.   A very early breakfast is pregnant with yawns, and may also be forgotten ; a very late one is unhappily curtailed.   Ten o'clock is an ideal to be striven after.   The host has to be studious not to invite two men who are "blues," or who are entered for the same examinations, or who are freshmen from the same school, which would be apt to produce treatises instead of conversation.   It is dangerous also to have two epigrammatists.   For that leads to a game of shuttlecock and battledore between the two, and of patience among the rest. . . .   He knows that four men incapable of these things are coming, and as he peeps from his bedroom to see that all is ready, he hears their steps and laughter echoing up the stairs. He is rapidly surveying them all in his mind, wondering how such excellent ingredients will mix, when they enter, having picked one another up by good fortune on the way, and already got rid of a possible tendency to talk about politics, weather, or dreams.   They discuss everything.   One who is bound to be a fellow starts on " the æsthetic value of dons."   One who has never left England offers a suggestive remark on Swiss scenery or the effect of palms against a sunrise in the Pacific. The transitions are indescribably rapid ; yet the link of merely an epigram or a laugh, or possibly the very sense of contrast and incongruity, makes the whole run on as some fine hedge of maple, hawthorn, holly, elm, beech, and wild cherry runs on, and is fine and nothing else, except to a botanist.   The talk is a play in five acts : each man is in turn a chorus.   But whether the subject be freshmen, or Disraeli, or Sancho Panza, or the English aristocracy, it is treated as it never was before.   Perhaps that is the result of the detached attitude of a number of very young men.   Perhaps it is because each in turn, of the five average men, is touched with genius temporarily by accretion from the other four.   One says a dull thing, another a silly thing, a third a rash thing, a fourth a vague thing, and straightway the fifth catches fire and blazes with something of the true light from heaven, and he not less than the rest is astonished. The spirit of the conversation is as different from the prandial spirit as shortbread from wedding cake.   It has neither the richness of that nor the frivolity of tea.

Oxford

The breakfast talker seems to depend very little on memory. He remembers fewer stories, less of the book he read on the night before, than at a later meal. He is thrown more entirely upon the resources of his own fantasy. The experience of sleep still lies like a great water between him and yesterday. In the cold, young, golden light, among the grey stones of the quadrangle, the brain, too, rejoices in its own life, and forgets to look before and after. Habit is weaker. He catches another glimpse of the "clouds of glory," if only in a mirage. He is renovated by the new day; and although by dinner-time he will have advanced to warmer sympathies and a more tranquil satisfaction, there will then be something more cynical in his indolent optimism than in the sharp but easily warded points of morning wit. . . . Of course, a breakfast party of men in training for the Torpids is another thing. That is a question of arithmetic. So, too, with a breakfast given formally to freshmen, which is mainly a question of time and stories about dons. Breakfasts with fellows are either of the best kind, or they are ceremonies. There are some colleges, where the fellows not only feel that there is no need of condescension, but they do not condescend: the elder is not expected to be preternaturally simple, nor the younger to be abstruse. In other colleges, such breakfasts of the great and small are sometimes farces and sometimes ceremonies. The don knows that the other's knowledge of the *Republic* is small; the undergraduate is equally aware of the fact: the one assumes that he has an index to the other's

The Oxford Day

mind ; the other that one so scathing in his opinion of essays will be the same in his treatment of little quips about the Colonial Secretary or accounts of pheasant-shooting in the Christmas vacation : one is determined to pounce ; the other not to be pounced upon. The scout who changes the dishes indicates whether it is a ceremony or a farce. If he smiles, it is the one ; if he does not, it is the other. Not everybody, indeed, in these colleges has the same misfortune, though any one may, as the young man who carefully prepared a paraphrase of one of the obscurest articles in the *Encyclopædia Britannica* and two brand new epigrams artfully inwoven, and served them up as he sat down at the breakfast table of the bursar, who smiled and commented moodily : " What a boon the *Encyclopædia* is to the tired man ! " But breakfast with even the best of dons has this disadvantage, that he can bring it to an end with a word ; so that his guest may afterwards be seen disconsolately reading a newspaper, and feeling that to have eaten food is hardly more to have breakfasted than to have dined.

Between nine and one o'clock the different species of Oxford kind are either within doors—sleeping, talk-ing, or working—or to be seen in various conditions of unrest ; observers and observed in the High, in pairs or singly ; and, if freshmen, either stately in scholars' gowns or apparently anxious to convince others that they have just picked up their commoners' gowns ; sauntering to the book-shops, or to look at a cricket pitch or a dog ; or hurrying to lectures with an earnestness that strangely disappears when they are seated and the lecture is begun.

In the stream of men there is one thin black line that is unwavering—the line of men, with white fillets of sacrifice under their chins, going to the examination Schools. This is the only place in the world where the plough is still wrought into a weapon of offence. They are under the care of a suitable, ferocious, wild man, who is one of the Old Guard of the opposition to women at Oxford; and in his bleak invitation to ladies, to proceed to their appointed rooms, lays terrible stress upon the word "women," as if it were a term of abuse in his strange tongue. He is partly responsible for the reply of an undergraduate to an American who asked, what might be the name of the buildings which he so admired and which made him feel at home?

"That," said the undergraduate, "is the Martyrs' Memorial."

"And who are those going in?"

"They are the Martyrs."

"But I thought they were burned three hundred years ago?"

"Sir," said the undergraduate impressively, "they are martyred twice daily."

"Well, I guess Oxford is very Middle Age and all that, but I didn't know it went so far as that": and the humane visitor went away, talking of agitation in the *New York Herald*.

Of all Oxford pastimes, that of going to the book-

The Oxford Day

shop after breakfast is one of the most wise. There the undergraduate meets the don whose lecture he has slighted ; in fact, he meets every one there, or escapes them, if he thinks fit, behind one of the tall piles. Some prefer leap-frog and hopping contests in the quadrangle. In some colleges they are said to read Plato under the trees in the morning : in others, it is to be presumed, in spite of the negligent capers of the wearers, that the hours are spent in choosing the necktie or waistcoat best suited to " flame in the forehead of the morning sky." Another amusement is to go to the Divinity School and see the Vice-Chancellor, seated between the two neat and restless proctors, conferring degrees. Near, and on either side of the daïs, the ladies are enjoying the scene. Below them sit dons who are to present members of their colleges, —a pale, superb, militant priest conspicuous among the rows of English gentlemen. Farther removed from authority is the Opposition, half a hundred undergraduates, who merrily applaud the perambulations of the mace-bearer or the deportment of their friends. Pale blue, and scarlet, and peach-coloured hoods make a brave contrast with the dead grey light and colourless stone of traceried ceiling and pillared walls, and the dim foliage of trees and ivy outside.

Lectures are a less stately pleasure. Some lecturers walk up and down the room as in a cage, and pause only for a more genial remark than usual, with uplifted gown and back to the blazing fire. Others laugh at their own jokes, or even at jokes which they leave unexpressed. Some are stern and impassioned : some appear to be proposing a health ; others, again, a vote of condolence. One came in clothed for travel, twenty minutes late, and after a few remarks, said that brevity was the most pardonable of the virtues, and that he had to catch a train ; and left. In the old days, Merton was famous for Schoolmen, Christ Church for poets, All Souls' for orators, Brasenose for disputants, and so on, says Fuller. That is not quite so now. Yet, as then, "all are eminent in some one kind or other," although the undergraduate does not always perceive it. Some are noted for research, some for views, some for condensation. An impartial observer once remarked that, "even when he is abridging an abridgment, an Oxford lecturer always had views." A scratching, coughing, whispering silence is respectfully observed. Once upon a time, a lady (not English) entered a famous hall, guide-book in hand, spectacles on nose ; went from place to place, contemplated all, and incurred only the amazement of the lecturer and the admiration of the audience. It is to be noticed that the audience of what M. Bardoux good-naturedly calls Monks, is in most cases far more interested in note-books than in the lecturer. Some will spend three consecutive hours in lecture rooms, and therein compile very curious anthologies. Even that does not conduce to enthusiasm ; and nobody in recent years has been electrified in an Oxford lecture room. "I have discovered," writes an outsider, "with much difficulty that there are two

The Oxford Day

classes in Oxford, the learned and the unlearned : my difficulty arose from the fact that the latter were without coarseness and the former without enthusiasm." And certainly in a city that loves to light bonfires, and is never more herself than when she is welcoming a guest, enthusiasm is astonishingly well concealed. It may be detected occasionally among gentlemen who are conducting East-Enders from quadrangle to quadrangle, or among those who like the ground-ivy beer at Lincoln College on Ascension Day, or among those who salute financiers and others in the act of becoming Doctors of Civil Law at the Encænia. It was said that some one unsuccessfully spread his gown as a carpet for the late Mr. Rhodes's feet : it is certain that some played upon him with little jets of truth very heartily, and asked Socratic questions, on that august occasion.

At luncheon there is, however, some enthusiasm ; not for the meal, which is commonly a stupid one, but for the long afternoon, to be spent in the parks, or on the river, or in the country, east to Wheatley, west to Fyfield. These matters, or the prospect of a long bookish afternoon indoors or (in the summer) under a willow on the Cherwell or Evenlode, encroach too absolutely upon luncheon to allow it to be anything more than an affair of knives and forks. As for the country, a man used frequently to walk so as to know all the fields for twenty miles on every side. But the walker is vanishing. Games take away their thousands ; bicycles their hundreds ; the motor car destroys twos and threes. On Sundays walking is almost fashionable ;

Oxford

on week-days it is in danger of becoming notorious as
the hall-mark of a "reading man." An uninteresting
youth was once asked, as a freshman, what exercise he
favoured, and replied, "I belong to the reading set and
go walks." The remark was generally considered to
lower him to the rank of the *Intellectuels*, or as the
"Guide Conversationelle" translates the word, the Prigs.
That guide, which appeared in the *J.C.R.* in June 1899,
is so characteristic in its humour that I cannot apologise
for quoting from it :—

GUIDE CONVERSATIONELLE DE L'ÉTRANGER À OXFORD

L'Américain.	The Anglo-Saxon.
L'Espion.	The proctor.
Le Chauvinisme.	Imperialism.
Le Morgue.	Self-respect.
Le Noble.	The good fellow.
Le Bourgeois pauvre.	The tosher [an unattached student]
Le Mauvais Repas.	Hall [dinner].
Le Repas.	The Grid [iron ; an Oxford social club].
Le Culte.	The Salvation Army.
Le Fou.	The earnest man.
Le Lion.	The don.
L'Intellectuel.	The Prig.
Merci.	——
Vous me devez cinq francs.	Oh ! it doesn't matter.
Je suis Athée.	I am broad.
Il est dans le mouvement.	He is a gentleman.
Il a manqué son coup.	I hate that man.
Suivre les cours.	Reading for a second.
Républicain de Vieille Roche.	Little Englander.
Opportuniste.	Conservative (*or*) Liberal.
Socialiste.	Radical.
Collectiviste.	Socialist.
Le vertu.	Our English way.
Etre vicieux.	To be out of it.

182

The Oxford Day

Il arrivera.
J'ai peur.
C'est faux.
Tu en as menti.
Abruti.

His father got that place.
Where's the good of ragging?
In some respects you are right.
Surely you must be mistaken.
My dear Sir!

The river (or *l'après midi*) is the new college of the nineteenth century. As an educational institution it is unquestioned. The college barges represent perhaps the most successful Oxford architecture of the age. Certainly it was a thought of no mean order which set that tapering line of gaudy galleys to heave and shimmer along the river-side, against a background of trees and grass, and themselves a background for the white figures of the oarsmen. It is a fine lesson in eloquence to listen to the coaches shouting reprimand and advice, in sentences one or two words long, to a panting crew. One can see the secret of English success in the meek reception which a number of hard-working, conscientious, abraded men give to the abuse of an idler on the bank. On the afternoon of the races all is changed. The man who yesterday shouted " Potato sacks ! " or " Pleasure boat ! " now screams " Well rowed all ! " Before and behind him flows all of the University that can run a mile. The faces of all are expressive in every inch ; all restraint of habit or decorum is gone for the time being. The racing boats make hardly a sound ; and for the most part the rowers hear not a sound from the bank, but only the click of their own rowlocks. Here and there a rattle is twirled ; a bell rings ; a pistol is fired ; and a pair or several pairs of boats creep into the side, winners and losers, and languidly watch the still competing boats as they pass. The noise of rattles, bells, pistols, whistles, bagpipes, frying-pans, and shouts can be heard in all the colleges and in the fields at Marston and Hinksey, where it has a kind of melody. Close at hand, it has a charm for the experienced tympanum : for in the cries of the victorious colleges the joy of victory is too great to allow of any discordant crow of mere triumph ; the cries of those about to be beaten are too determined to have in them anything of hate. Such is the devout enthusiasm of the runners on the bank that if their own college boat is bumped they will sometimes run on to cheer the next boat that passes. The mysteries of harmony are never so wonderful as when, opposite the barge of a college that has made its bump, the sound of a hundred voices and a hundred instruments goes up, from dons, clergymen, old members of the college, future bishops, governors, brewers, schoolmasters, literary men, all looking very much the same, and in their pride of college forgetting all other pride. "If the next great prophet comes in knickerbockers, with good legs and a megaphone, he will be received in Oxford," says one as he leaves the river. "Was a prophet possible? Would he be a warrior, or an orator, or a quiet actor and persuader? Out of the wilderness, or out of the slum?" Such were the questions asked. "In any case he would not be listened to in Oxford," thought one. "Why not? provided his accent was good," thought another. "Comfort yourself," said a third ; "some one would ask at hall table what school he came

The Oxford Day

from ; the question would go round ; and the prophet would retreat from the refrigerator." "But suppose him a sort of Kipling, twenty or thirty feet broader every way——"

"Send up some buttered crumpets and slow poison" was the epitaph of the conversation, which was, after all, between children of a cynical age and in the hour of tea. But there is many a true thing said at tea in Oxford. The hours from four to seven are nothing if not critical. It is an irresponsible, frivolous time, and an interregnum between the tyranny of exercise and the tyranny of food. Nothing is now commended ; yet nothing is envied. I suspect that some of the causes of the University love of parody might be found by an investigator in the Oxford tea. Over his crumpet or "slow poison" the undergraduate who is no wiser than he should be legislates for the world, settles even higher matters, and smilingly accepts a viceroyalty from Providence. With some it is a festival of Slang— venerable goddess ! I have heard a philologist trace a little Oxford phrase to the thieves of Manchester a century ago or more. Now he plans profound or witty speeches for the Union, devises "rags" and rebellions, and writes for the undergraduate magazines, and has his revenge in a few well-chosen words upon coaches, dons, captains of football, and all forms of Pomposity, Dulness, and Good Sense. "Common-sense," says one, "is nonsense *à la mode*." He luxuriates in the criticism of life, and blossoms with epigrams. He says in his heart, "In much wisdom is much grief : and he that increaseth knowledge increaseth sorrow," and sets himself to make sayings which, if not truer than proverbs, are funnier. Others prowl : *i.e.* they go through that promiscuous calling upon acquaintances which is the bane of half its beneficiaries. Some of these prowlers seem to live by this kind of canvassing—thieves of others' time and generous givers of their own. They will boast of having taken twenty teas in one afternoon. But on Sunday comes their judgment. They wear a soberer aspect on their way to the drawing-rooms of Oxford hostesses. In the comfortable chairs sit the incurable habitués—cold, saturnine spectators, or impudent, stiff-hearted epigrammatists, handing round at regular intervals neat slices from the massy joints of their erudition or their wit. They smile sadly and yet complacently over their tea-cups as the prowler enters. They wait until the victim is in right position, viz. with a perfectly true remark about the weather, or Sunday, or sport, or dentists ; and then suddenly "slit the thin-spun life" with an unseasonable query or corroboration. The hostess smiles imperceptibly. In a few moments the prowler is gone. "Mr.——," says the hostess, "you pronounce the sweetest obituaries I ever meet, but I have never known you to pronounce them over the deceased."

> Here glow the lamps,
> And teaspoons clatter to the cosy hum
> Of scientific circles. Here resounds
> The football field with its discordant train,
> The crowd that cheers but not discriminates. . . .

There are also teas with the young, the beautiful,

and the virtuous in the plain and exclusive northernmost haunts of learning in Oxford. The University could not well do without their sweet influences. Yet if men, in their company, are often better than themselves, as is only right, they are perhaps less than themselves. Also, in wit carnivals, it is permitted to women to use all kinds of weapons, from a sigh to a tea-urn ; to men they are not permitted, although they have nothing sharper or more rankling in their armoury. Hence, on the part of generous women, a sort of pity, and on the part of men some timidity and (short of rudeness) ter-giversation. And I am not privileged to give an account of a real Somerville tea.

But it is a thing impossible to praise in rhyme or prose the pleasures of tea at Oxford—perhaps especially in autumn, as the sun is setting after rain—when a man knows not whether it is pleasanter to be rained upon at Cumnor, or to be dried again by his fire—and the bells are ringing.

> Not that Nepenthes which the wife of Thone
> In Egypt gave to Jove-born Helena,
> Is of such power to stir up joy as this,
> To life so friendly.

Perhaps, as you light candles, and ask, "What is warmth without light?" your companion replies, "A minor poet"; and when you ask again in irritation, "What is light without warmth?" he is ready with, "An edition of Tennyson with notes." And not even the recollection of such things and worse can spoil the charm of Oxford tea. Then it is that the homeliness of Oxford is dearest. And what a carnival of contrasts in men and manners can be seen in a little room. "Oxford," writes the *Oxford Spectator*,—

Oxford is a stage,
And all the men in residence are players :
They have their exeats and examinations ;
And one man in his time plays many parts,
His acts being seven ages. At first the Freshman,
Stumbling and stuttering in his tutor's rooms.
And then the aspiring Classman, with white tie
And shy, desponding face, creeping along
Unwilling to the Schools. Then, at the Union,
Spouting like Fury, with some woeful twaddle
Upon the "Crisis." Then a Billiard-player,
Full of strange oaths, a keen and cunning card,
Clever in cannons, sudden and quick at hazards,
Seeking a billiard reputation
Even in the pocket's mouth. And then the Fellow,
His fair, round forehead with hard furrows lined,
With weakened eyes and beard of doubtful growth,
Crammed with old lore of useless application,
And so he plays his part. The sixth age shifts
Into the lean and study-worn Professor,
With spectacles on nose and class at side ;
His youthful nose has grown a world too large
For his shrunk face ; and his big, manly voice,
Turning again towards childish treble, pipes
And whistles in his sound. Last scene of all,
That ends this strange, eventful history
In utter donnishness and mere nonentity,
Without respect, or tact, or taste, or anything.

I said that undergraduate magazine humour was a tea-table flower. I should have said that it flowers at tea and is harvested after dinner. The penning of it is a nocturnal occupation, and the best wit is sometimes the result of that pregnant nervousness which comes from competing with time. It was until very lately

The Oxford Day

a tradition that undergraduate journalism should be anonymous. Of many good and feeble things the authorship will now probably never be known. "Hath the rain a father? or who hath begotten the drops of dew?" And it is an odd thing that so few reputations have been promised or made therein. Probably the writers of the Cambridge *Light Green* and the "Lambkin Papers" in the *J.C.R.* of Oxford have alone not only shown but fulfilled their promise in contributions to an undergraduate periodical. The explanation is that the cleverest men are content to produce either parody or what is narrowly topical, and both of these are usually born in their graves. "Parody," said a don, "is always with us, and nearly always against us." Parody and its companions are, in fact, a sort of unofficial bull-dogs, that persecute all forms of bad, and even good, behaviour which do not come within the proctor's jurisdiction. The proctor is a favourite victim. "O vestment of velvet and virtue," runs an obvious parody in the *Shotover Papers* of 1874, by "Gamble Gold,"—

> O vestment of velvet and virtue,
>   O venemous victors of vice,
> Who hurt men who never have hurt you,
>   Oh, calm, cruel, colder than ice.
> Why wilfully wage ye this war? is
>   Pure pity purged out of your breast?
> O purse-prigging Procuratores,
>   O pitiless pest!

The wise fool, the foolish wise man, the impostor, and the ungainly fanatic, are all game to the undergraduate

189

satirist. "We draw our bow at a venture," he writes; "so look to it, don and undergraduate, boating men and reading men; look to it, O Union orators, statesmen of the future; look to it, ye patrons of St. Philip's and St. Aldate's; look to it, ye loungers in the Parks; look to it, ye Proctors, and thou, O Vice-Chancellor, see that your harness be well fitted, that between its joints no arrow shall pierce. Our aim is careless, but perhaps it may strike deep; if we cannot smite a king we shall contentedly wing a freshman." Not seldom this note of Titanic defiance is struck by the freshman himself. If he cannot be an example of what is most subtle in literature or most brilliant in life, he will peacefully consent to be in his own person a warning against the commonplace. He is, indeed, very often among the parodists, although as a rule he does not get beyond imitation. Perhaps the large percentage of parodists will account for that timidity of poets which has left Cambridge almost without a tribute from its countless band. The gay, sarcastic man who dines next to you, or is a fellow-officer at the Union, is bound to hear of your serious follies in print, and will as infallibly make that an excuse for rushing into print himself. I have even heard it seriously urged that the number of critics in Oxford accounts for the silence of nearly every one else, and that not the irresponsible undergraduate alone blasts the blossoms of wisdom while he takes the sting out of foolishness. A cautious use of high teas might be recommended as a step towards seriousness.

The Oxford Day

Some, even to-day, fly speedily from tea to work. Upon others, and in some degree upon these, dinner lays a cheerful hand in anticipation. The optimist becomes "happier and wiser both." The very pessimist rises at least to a cynic. Under the head of dinner I include, first and least, the discussion of the cook's poetry and prose, if one may be permitted to make the distinction, since his joints have been called "poems in prose"; second, the feast of reason, etc.; third, those acts of pleasure or duty which came naturally to the wise diner. The first two are hardly distinct acts. "We *devour*," says Leigh Hunt, "wit and argument, and *discuss* a turkey and chine." The word "dinner" was once derived from the Greek word for terrible, and was held to imply not so much its terrors for the after-dinner speaker, as for the man who came simply to eat. Most Oxford colleges have accordingly an elaborate and forcible set of rules for humiliating the sordid man. In old days he apparently quoted from the Bible, which every one knew, just as every one knows the *Times* to-day; and consequently a quotation from the Bible was punished along with puns, quotations from Latin and Greek, and oaths. As unbecoming to a feast of reason, flannels and other clothes belonging to the barbaric hours of life are forbidden. The unpunctuality of such as obviously come only to devour is treated in the same way. Gross inadvertence or apparent physical incapacity to do anything but eat have also been punished in gentlemen both punctual and suitably clothed; but these and other excesses of

191

virtuous intention are not always sanctioned by the High Table. The punishment usually takes the form of a fine to the extent of two quarts of beer, which the sufferer has to put in circulation among his judges. Punning, too, is attacked. It was time that the pun should go. It was becoming too perfect, and a monopoly of the mathematical mind. Two hundred years ago men laughed at this :—"A chaplain in the University of Oxford, having one leg bigger than the other, was told that his legs might be *chaplains* too, for they were never like to be *fellows*." To-day, it is doubtful whether it would be honoured by the fine or "sconce." Yet the pun has in a sense been supplanted not very worthily by the "spoonerism." That, too, has become a very solemn affair. It is in the hands of calculating prodigies, and men are expected to laugh at "pictures defeated" instead of "features depicted" and the like. It smacks of the logic required for a pass degree, while the old puns *sentent plus le vin que l'huile*. Yet the spoonerism is venerable in years ; and Anthony Wood records among his pieces of humour the saying of Dr. Ratcliff of Brasenose, that "a proud man will buy a dagger or die a beggar." Nor is the anecdote extinct, as one may learn from the laughter at any High Table, where it is known that men do not discuss ontology. Oxford humour, at and after dinner, may be divided under these heads :—

(1) The Rag.
(2) The Epigram.
(3) Humour.

The Oxford Day

The first, saving when it amounts to house-breaking or assault, or should endanger the perpetrator under the last Licensing Act, consists in the thoughtful preparation and execution of something unexpected for the benefit of an offending person, or in the elaboration of something visibly and audibly funny for fun's sake at the expense of the artists alone. It was "a rag," for example, two hundred and fifty years ago, as also more recently, to make a various and crowded ceremony of the enforced exit of a popular undergraduate. The hero may be mounted on a hearse or a steam-roller, and proceed with stately accompaniment. Or he may go in pink with a pack of bull-dogs, and whips dressed as proctors, to the tune of "The Conquering Hero." Some prefer twenty-four barrel-organs, if obtainable. But the "rag" is a branch of decorative art that deserves a volume with illustrations. No one who has not studied it can guess at the beautiful work which is devoted to the conversion of a gentleman's bedroom into a sitting-room. Any one who would teach us how divine a thing the rag can be made, would be heartily thanked. I may remark, in passing, that it gives full play to the intellect,—is, in fact, a counterpart to the occupations of the schoolmen, and is neither less practical nor less ingenious, and reaches its highest perfection in the hands of scholars who can do nothing without remembering Plato, and say nothing without remembering Aristophanes. Lest I should be suspected of not being on the side of the angels in recent controversy, I will give no examples, save a trifling one

which has just been recalled for me by a volume of
Hazlitt. We made a supper party of six with Corydon,
our host at —— in Oxford. His gestures (particularly
a gracious way of bowing his head as he smiled) had a
magic that quickly made our number seem inevitable
and right. Very soon all were talking eagerly in
harmonious alternation. A choicely laden board of
cold viands, which none seemed to have noticed, stood
unvisited, and was finally cleared. Corydon was speaking (of nothing in the least important) when the servant
carried in a strange but dainty course of little, fine old
books that sent the conversation happily into every
nook that rivers from Helicon visit. Again and again
came in dishes of the same character, for which
Corydon's purse and library had been ransacked. The
wealth of how many provinces — to use an honoured
phrase — had gone to the preparation of that meal!
"And by the way, I have some cold fowls and wine
and fruit ready," the host said suddenly. . . . One
found that Shelley and champagne were good bosom
friends ; another that a compôte of port, Montaigne,
and pomegranate was incomparable. . . . This Hazlitt
also was at that excellent supper and "rag." Nor can
I omit a mention of the strong sculptor who strove all
night in the midst of a wintry quadrangle, in order to
astonish the college with a snow statue of the most
jovial fellow of the society, with a cigar between his
teeth and a bottle in each hand. Mr. Godley has sung
of a more boisterous rag, "the raid the Saxon made
on the Cymru men," which was in this way :—

The Oxford Day

Mist upon the marches lay, dark the night and late,
Came the bands of Saxondom, knocking at a gate,—
Mr. Jones the person was whom they came to see—
He, they said, had courteously asked them in to tea.

Did they, when that college gate open wide was thrown,
Go and see the gentleman, as they should have done ?
No : in Impropriety's indecorous tones
(Quite unmeet for tea-parties) loud they shouted "Jones!"

Straightway did a multitude answer to their call—
Un, dau, tri, pedwar, pump, chwech—Mr. Joneses all—
Loud as Lliwedd's echoes ring all asserted, "We
Never asked these roistering Saesnegs in to tea!"

Like the waves of Anglesey, crashing on the coast,
Came the Cymru cohorts then : countless was their host :
Retribution stern and swift evermore assails
Him who dares to trifle with gallant little Wales. . . .

One who might be supposed to know said in
1899 that where a Cambridge man would know an
article from the *Encyclopædia Britannica* by heart, an
Oxford man would abridge it in an epigram ; and
there, he contended, was a difference and a distinction.
But the epigram is said to be dying. It were greatly
to be regretted, if that were true, since the epigram
was the handsomest medium ever chosen by inexperience for its own expression. As poetry is a criticism
of life by livers, so the epigram is a criticism of life by
those who have not lived. It used to be the toga of
the infant prodigy at Oxford. "If only life were a
dream, and I could afford hansoms!" or "A little
Jowett is a dangerous thing!" used to pass muster in
a crowd of epigrams. But I seemed to see the skirt of

the departing epigram this year, when a young man
exclaimed that he had discovered that, "After all, life
is the thing," in a discussion concerning conduct and
literature : and the shock was hardly lessened by the
critical repartee that the remark was "not only true
but inadequate." A few years ago smaller notions than
that were not allowed to go into the world without
their fashionable suit. That was the epigram. It was
a verbal parallel to legerdemain. The quickness of the
fancy deceived the brain : or rather the brain made it
a point of courtesy to be deceived. For there was a
kindly conspiracy between the speaker and the hearer
in the matter of epigrams. A certain degree of skill
was expected of the latter, who knew almost infallibly
whether a saying was an epigram, just as he would have
known a hearse or a skiff. It was the jingling bell
which every one but the exceptionally clever wore in his
cap, to prove that he aspired to talk. All were epigrammatists, and regarded as alien nothing epigrammatical.
When "Lady Windermere's Fan" was played at
Oxford, even those who had not heard them before
laughed at the epigrams in the Club scene. One such
remarked to a persevering imitator of Wilde : "The
epigrams in 'Lady Windermere' were a faint echo of
yourself." But these are other times, and when the
same youth, bald and still young, very recently ventured
to clothe a little truism archaically, the curate next to
him touched a note of horror mingled with contempt
as he said, "That sounded like an epigram." In one
respect an Oxford dinner is the better for the absence

The Oxford Day

of epigram. The machine-made article is impossible. It used to be as ineffectual as the prayers of Thibet. A man might be seen, forgetful of the world, nursing his faculties from soup to ice, in the gestation of an epigram. Thus it tended to cast a shadow over conversation, and to replace the genial, slow, and whist-like alternations of good talk with the sudden follies of snap or the violences of bridge. Breakfast itself was sometimes made the occasion of duels, with a thrust and parry not oftener than twice in a course. A man would come melancholy to luncheon because he had not hit upon a good thing in the lecture which preceded it. Nevertheless, there was something to be said for the manufacture, if not for the manufacturer. His epigrams could be repeated *spontaneously* by another. Thus an elderly morose undergraduate, unable to knot a bow, would one day ejaculate at the wrong moment: "A woman is never too stupid to be loved, nor too clever to love." The next evening a simple and dashing boy would make a hit with it, by nice judgment of time and place. Much applause was sometimes accorded to the wit of laborious, obscure young men who were content to father their offspring upon the illustrious. Thus, one undergraduate was once found slaving at an original work, entitled "Addenda to the Posthumous Humour of the late Master of Balliol."

Of humour, the third divison, there is nothing to be said. It has been met with at the Union, in spite of the notice :—

Oxford

Lost !
A sense of humour
by the following gentlemen——
They will take in exchange early numbers of *Sword and Trowel* or a selection
of hatbands.

For the most part, the heavier vices and lighter virtues
of speech are said to flourish there. " It is a pity," said
a critic of the Union, " that so many ingenious youths
should disarm themselves by pretending to be in the
House of Commons, which they rival as a club." A
Frenchman has said that its histrionic wealth at one
time equalled the house of Molière. Indeed, as a home
of comedy it is the most amusing and accomplished in
Oxford ; and on that account, probably, the public
theatre seldom provides anything but opera and farce.
A bland, clever youth, stooping like a candle in hot
July—his body and a scroll of foolscap quivering with
emotion, as he suggests to a smiling house that the
Conservative party should bury its differences under the
sole management of Mr. Redmond : a stiff, small,
heroic figure—with a mouth that might sway armies,
a voice as sweet as Helicon, as irresistible and continuous
as Niagara—pouring forth praise of the English aristocracy and the Independent Labour Party, to a house
that believes or disbelieves, and applauds : a minute,
tormented skeleton, acrobatic and ungainly, so eloquent
on the futility of Parliament, that he might govern the
Empire, if he could govern himself : one who is not
really comfortable without a cigarette, yet awes the
house by his superb complacency, as he utters now and

then a languid epigram about the Irish peasantry or indigo, in the brief intervals of an apparent colloquy with himself :—these and a multitude of the fervid, the weighty, the listless, the perky, and the dull, are among the Union orators of yesterday. " I went to the Union to be amused," says one. "They were debating a question of literature. A brilliant man opened ; a learned opposed. Others followed—some for, some against, the motion ; others again made observations. I was not disappointed. I was edified. There was no research. There was little originality. But there was a dazzling simplicity and lucidity, and an extraordinary power of treating controversially the profoundest matters as if they were common knowledge ; above all, the reserved gestures, the self-control, were dignified, and made me believe that I was listening to the opinions of an assembly of middle-aged men of the world, and not a handful of students not yet past their majority." But the glories of Union oratory are weekly : the theatre is consequently a favourite evening lounge ; some even prefer it on Thursdays. It is noticeable that the house is more familiar than elsewhere in its praise or disapproval of the players. Half a dozen in the dress circle will hold a (rather one-sided) conversation with the stage for half an evening. It is also customary, and especially on Saturdays, for the audience to sing the choruses of songs to their taste many times over, and then to revive them in the quiet streets. Banquets, and the reception given to the speeches of actors and managers, and the nature of those speeches as well, prove the hearty fellowship between University and stage. It has long been so. "At a stage play in Oxford," says one old author, "(at the King's Arms in Holywell) a Cornishman was brought in to wrestle with three Welshmen, one after another, and when he had worsted them all, he called out, as his part was, Have you any more Welshmen? Which words one of Jesus College took in such indignation that he leaped upon the stage and threw the player in earnest." It must be admitted, however, that such familiarities on the stage itself are now unknown.

To a stranger walking from the Union or the theatre, after Tom has sounded the ideal hour of studious retirement, Oxford might well appear to be a nest of singing birds. The windows of brilliantly lighted rooms, with curtains frequently undrawn, in dwelling-house or college, reveal rows of backs and rows of faces, with here one at a piano and there one standing beside, singing lustily, while the rest try with more or less success to concentrate their talents upon the chorus : probably they are singing something from *Gaudeamus*, *Scarlet and Blue*, or other song-books for students, soldiers, and sailors ; or, it may be, a folk song that has never come into print. Sometimes, in the later evening, the singing is not so beautiful. For here those sing who never sang before, and those who used to sing now sing the more. Perhaps only the broadest-minded lover of grotesque contrasts will care for the ballads flung to the brightening moon among the battlements and towers. But the others should not judge harshly or with haste. These are but part of the motley in which learning clothes itself. Much sound and fury is here no proof of deep-seated folly ; nor quietness, of study ; nor are a man's age, dignity, and accomplishments in mathematical proportion to the demureness of his deportment. I notice on one little tankard these philosophies in brief, scrawled with a broken pen :—

> Ah ! who would lose thee,
> When we no more can use or even abuse thee ?

> ΠΑΝΤΑ ΡΕΙ.

> Qui vit sans folie n'est pas si sage qu'il croit.

> The old is better.

> How dull it is to pause, to make an end,
> To rust unburnished, not to shine in use.

> ΜΙΣΕΩ ΜΝΑΜΟΝΑ ΣΥΜΠΟΤΑΝ

> Assiduitate non desidia.

> Too much study is sloth.

> Desine fata deum flecti sperare precando.

> Quittez le long espoir et les vastes pensées.

And though some are evidently framed with an eye confined to the tankard, how applicable all are to the shining pewter and life itself !

You shall be in one small sitting-room, on an evening, while in one corner a ditty from the *Studentenlieder* is hummed ; in another, Hagen's *Carmina Medii Ævi* or W. B. Yeats or Marlowe is declaimed ; in another, you shall hear ghosts or sports discussed ; in a fourth, the orthodoxy of the *Inferno* : yet the whole company shall be one in spirit. And the same in another such room—where a dozen men are divided into groups around three of the number who are reading, for discussion, the rules of the Salvation Army, the *Anthologia Planudea*, and a Blue Book.

At the top of an adjacent staircase there is a lonely gentleman eating strawberries and cream, and thinking about wall-paper ; or one like a gnome, amidst innumerable books,—his floor strewn with notes, phrases, queries,—writing a prize essay ; or one reading law, with his newly-presented football cap on his head ; one reading Kipling and training a meerschaum ; one alternately reading the *Organon* of Aristotle and quoting verbatim from Edgar Allen Poe to admiring workers at the same text ; or one digesting opium, and now and then looking for five minutes at one or other of a huge pile of books at his side—Paul Verlaine, Marlowe, Jeremy Taylor, the *Odyssey*, Ariosto, and Pater. The staircases creak or clatter with the footsteps of men going up and down, to and from these rooms. Outside one or two sets of rooms the great outer door—the " oak "—is fastened, a signal that the owner wishes to be undisturbed, and practically an invitation to trials of strength with heel and shoulder from the passer-by. In the faintly lighted quadrangles, men are hurrying, or sauntering, or resting on the grass among the trees. Perhaps there is a light in the college hall. The sound of a castanet dance played by a band —or a song—comes through the window. The music

The Oxford Day

grows wilder. The chorus swallows up the song. There are half a dozen conductors beating time, among the crowded benches of the audience. The small lights are but stains upon the air, which is composed of cigar and cigarette smoke. Mirth is eloquently expressed in every way, from laughter to a snore. The candles begin to fall from the brackets ; the seats are carried out ; and, to a still wilder tune, two hundred men join hands and dance. The band is given no rest : in fact, they are unable to rest, and the same glow sits in their cheeks. But in the darkness they slip away. For all the candles are out, and there is a bonfire making red weals upon the grey walls ; then another dance ; and a hundred times, " Auld lang syne," until the college is quiet, and but rarely a light is seen through curtains and over battlements : and the long Oxford night begins. *Large reponens*, we build up the fire. If it be autumn, we will hardly permit it ever to go out, thus consoling ourselves for the transitory glow of the sun, and fantastically handing on the sunsets of many summers and the dawns of many springs, in that constant flame. Sitting before it, we seem to evolve a fiery myth, and think that Apollo and Arthur and other "solar" heroes more probably leapt radiant from just such a fire before the eyes of more puissant dreamers in the old time. The light creeps along the wall, fingering title after title of our books. They are silently preluding to a second spring, when poets shall sing instead of birds, and we shall gather old fragrant flowers, not from groves, but from books. We see coming a long, new summer, a bookish summer, when we shall rest by olive and holm oak and palm and cypress, and not leave our chairs—a summer of evenings, with tropic warmth, no cloud overhead, and skies of what hue we please.

> There many Minstrales maken melody,
> To drive away the dull Melancholy,
> And many Bardes, that to the trembling chord
> Can tune their timely voices cunningly :
> And many Chroniclers, that can record
> Old loves and warres for Ladies doen by many a Lord.

A certain Italian poet used " to retire to bed for the winter." He had some wisdom, and we will follow him in spirit ; but, having Oxford rooms and Oxford armchairs, that were not dreamed of in his philosophy, we need not stay abed. Few of the costless luxuries are dearer than the hour's sleep amidst the last chapter of the night, while the fire is crumbling, grey, and murmurous, as if it talked in its sleep. The tenderest of Oxford poets knew these nights :—

> About the august and ancient *Square*
> Cries the wild wind ; and through the air,
> The blue night air, blows keen and chill ;
> Else, all the night sleeps, all is still.
> Now the lone *Square* is blind with gloom,
> A cloudy moonlight plays, and falls
> In glory upon *Bodley's* walls :
> Now, wildlier yet, while moonlight pales,
> Storm the tumultuary gales.
> O rare divinity of Night !
> Season of undisturbed delight :
> Glad interspace of day and day !
> Without, an world of winds at play :
> Within, I hear what dead friends say.

The Oxford Day

Blow, winds ! and round that perfect *Dome*
Wail as you will, and sweep, and roam :
Above *Saint Mary's* carven home,
Struggle and smite to your desire
The sainted watchers on her spire :
Or in the distance vex your power
Upon mine own *New College* tower :
You hurt not these !   On me and mine
Clear candlelights in quiet shine :
My fire lives yet ! nor have I done
With *Smollett*, nor with *Richardson :*
With, gentlest of the martyrs ! *Lamb,*
Whose lover I, long lover, am :
With *Gray*, where gracious spirit knew
The sorrows of arts lonely few. . . .

And it is day once more ; and beauty, the one thing
in Oxford that grows not old, seems a new-born, joyous
thing, to a late watcher who looks out and sees the
light first falling on dewy spires.

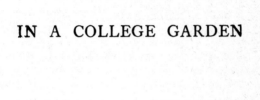

IN A COLLEGE GARDEN

CHAPTER VII

IN A COLLEGE GARDEN

IN spring, when it rained, says Aubrey, Lord Bacon used to go into the fields in an open coach, "to receive the benefit of irrigation, which he was wont to say was very wholesome because of the nitre in the aire, and the universal spirit of the world." Nor is it difficult in a college garden to associate the diverse ceremonial of Nature with the moods and great days of men. What, for example, can lay such fostering hands upon the spirit that has grown callous in the undecipherable sound of cities, as the grey February clouds that emerge from the sky hardly more than the lines in mother-of-pearl or the grain of a chestnut? I have thought,—in that garden,—that we are neglectful of the powers of herb and flower to educate the soul, and that the magical herbalists were nobly guessing at difficult truths when they strove to find a "virtue" in every product of lawn and sedge. There is a polarity between the genius of certain places and certain temperaments ; our "genial air" or natal atmosphere is, we may think, enriched by the soul of innumerable plants, beyond the neighbourhood of which some people are never quite *themselves*. And this college garden of smooth, shining lawn, and trees that seem more than trees in their close old friendship with grey masonry, has a singular aptness to—I had almost said a singular knowledge of—those who have first been aware of beauty in its shade. "If there be aught in heredity, I must perforce love gardens ; and until the topographer of Eden shall arise, I have set my heart on this." So says a theologian, one of its adornments in academic black and white.

Old and storied as it is, the garden has a whole volume of subtleties by which it avails itself of the tricks of the elements. Nothing could be more romantic than its grouping and contrasted lights when a great, tawny September moon leans—as if pensively at watch—upon the garden wall. No garden is so fortunate in retaining its splendour when summer brusquely departs, or so rich in the idiom of green leaves when the dewy charities of the south wind are at last accepted. None so happily assists the music and laughter and lamps of some festivity. And when in February the heavy rain bubbles at the foot of the trees, and spins a shifting veil about their height and over the grass, it seems to reveal more than it conceals. The loneliness of the place becomes intense, as if one were hidden far back in time, and one's self an anachronism. It is a return to Nature. The whole becomes primeval ; and it is hard to throw off the illusion of being deep in woods and in some potent presence—

In a College Garden

Hoc nemus . . .
Quis deus incertum est, habitat deus.

At such times the folded gloom gives up the tale of the past most willingly.

The casual stranger sees little in the garden but neatness and repose. He may notice how luckily the few trees occur, and what warmth the shrubbery bestows, when they are black with rain and the crocus petals are spilt in silence. In a little while he may be privileged to learn what a great space for the eye, and especially for the imagination, the unknown gardener has contrived out of a few roods of high-walled grass. He will perhaps end by remarking that an acre is more than so many square yards, and by supposing that it is unique because it is academic.

But it is no merely academic charm that keeps him there, whether the sun in October is so bright on the frosty grass that the dead leaves disappear when they fall,—or on a spring evening the great chestnut expands ; its beauty and magnitude are as things newly and triumphantly acquired ; and it fills the whole space of sky, and in a few minutes the constellations hang in its branches.

It is rather perfect than academic ; a garden of which the most would say that, after their own, it is the best. Its shape and size are accidents, for it embraces the sites of an old hall, a graveyard, and an orchard of Elizabeth's time ; and the expert mole might here and there discover traces of a dozen successive fashions since it was clipped and carved by a dialist and peppered with tulips. But a thoughtful conservatism and a partnership between many generations have given it an indubitable style. The place has, as it were, a nationality, and the inevitable boundaries are apparently the finishing-strokes of the picture and not its aboriginal frame. Yet it is no natural garden into which any one may stroll and scatter the ends of cigarettes. A strong customary law is expressed by the very aspect of the place. Hence, part of it is still sacred to the statelier leisure of the dons. Hence, where any one can go, whether by right, or from a lack of beadles, it is the good fortune of every one to find himself alone when he reaches the spot. Even so, the trees have never quite their just tribute of dignity and ceremonial. They would be pleased to welcome back the days when Shenstone could only visit Jago secretly, because he wore a servitor's gown ; when even Gibbon remembered with satisfaction " the velvet cap and silk gown which distinguish a gentleman commoner from a plebeian student " ; and when, within living memory, the " correct thing for the quiet, gentlemanly under-graduate was a black frock-coat and tall hat, with the neatest of gloves and boots," on his country walk. The garden, when its borders were in scrolls, knots, and volutes, was certainly not among

> The less ambitious Pleasures found
> Beneath the *Liceat* of an humble Bob,

but was chiefly honoured by those who had graduated into a grizzled wig " with feathery pride,"—Mr. Rake-

In a College Garden

well of Queen's or Beau Trifle of Christ Church, or the ornate gentleman who are depicted in Ackerman,—and by dons who had never lost their self-respect by the scandal of keeping the company of undergraduates. When Latin was the language of conversation at dinner and supper, the trees looked their best. The change came, perhaps, in the days of the President who went about the world muttering *Mors omnibus communis*, or when our grandfathers made the gravel shriek with their armchair races across the quadrangles ; for in those days, according to an authority on roses, under-graduates either read, or hunted, or drove, or rowed, or walked (*i.e.* up and down the High). The pile of the lawn continued to deepen, and the trees to write new legends upon the sky.

The limes are in number equal to the fellows of the college, and, with the great warden horse-chestnut and the lesser trees, make up a solemn and wise society. They waste no time. Now and then they talk a little, and when one talks, the others follow ; but as a rule the wryneck or the jackdaw talks instead ; and with them it seems to be near the end of the day, nothing remaining save *benedictus benedicat*. In the angriest gale and in the scarcely grass-moving air of twilight the cypresses nod almost without sound. They are sentinels, unarmed, powerful in their unknown watch-word, solemn and important as negroes born in the days of Haroun Alraschid. They say the last word on calm. And so old —— goes there often, to remember the great days of the college fifty years ago, and, looking

priest-like with his natural tonsure and black long
gown, seems to worship some unpermitted graven image
among the shadows. When *he* is in the garden, the
intruder may see a complete piece of mediæval Oxford ;
for the louvre, and the line of roofs, and the mullioned
windows are, from that point of view, as they were in
the founder's time.

At the feet of the trees are the flowers of the seasons
in their order. Here and there the precious dark earth
is visible, adding a charm to the pale green stems and
leaves and the splendid or thoughtful hues of blossom.
The flower borders and plots carve the turf into such a
shape that it seems a great quiet monster at rest. One
step ahead the grass is undivided, enamelled turf :
underfoot, the innumerable blades have each a colour, a
movement, a fragrance of their own,—as when one
enters a crowd, that had seemed merely a crowd, and
finds in it no two alike.

On one side is the shrubbery, of all the hues of the
kingdom of green. Underneath the shrubs the gloom
is a presence. The interlacing branches are as the
bars of its cage. You watch and watch—like children
who have found the lion's cage, but the lion invisible—
until gradually, pleased and still awed, you see that the
caged thing is—nothingness, in all its shadowy pomp
and immeasurable power. Seated there, you could
swear that the darkness was moving about, treading the
boundaries. When I first saw it, it was a thing as new
and strange as if I had seen the world before the sun,
and withdrawing my eyes and looking at the fresh limes

In a College Garden

was like beholding the light of the first dawn arriving at Eden. And in the evening that accumulated gloom raised the whole question between silence and speech, and did not answer it. The song of the blackbird is heard, cushioned among the sleepy cooings of doves. And when they cease, how fine is the silence! When they revive, how fine is the song! For the silence seems to appropriate and not to destroy the song. The blackbird, too, seems to appropriate and make much of the silence when he sings. The long meditations of the gowned and ungowned therein are not of less account because the only tangible result is the perfect beheading of dandelions as they walk to and fro.

> How shall I name you, immortal, mild, proud shadows?
> I only know that all we know comes from you,
> And that you come from Eden on flying feet.
> Is Eden far away, or do you hide
> From human thought, as hares and mice and coneys
> That run before the reaping-hook and lie
> In the last ridge of the barley? Do our woods
> And winds and ponds cover more quiet woods,
> More shining winds, more star-glimmering ponds?
> Is Eden out of time and out of space?
> And do you gather about us when pale light
> Shining on water and fallen among leaves,
> And winds blowing from flowers, and whirr of feathers,
> And the green quiet, have uplifted the heart?

Not often can the most academic dreamer see Faunus among those trees or Daphne in the laurel again.

On the grass the shadows of the roof, and later, of a tree, make time an alluring toy. The shadow is cut in finer and sharper angles than the roofs make, in the rich, hazy, Oxford light.

Oxford

To walk round about the garden twice could not occupy an hour of the most tranquil or gouty human life, even if you stayed to see the toadflaxes and ferns in the wall, to note the shape of the trees, and admire how the changing sun patronises space after space of the college buildings. Yet no maze or boundless moor could give a greater pleasure of seclusion and security. Not in vain has it served many academic generations as a sweet and melodious ante-chamber of the unseen. For, as an old book grows the richer to the wise reader, for the porings of its dead owners in past years, so these trees and this lawn have been enriched. Their roots are deep in more than earth. Their crests traffic with more than the doves and the blue air. There is surely no other garden so fit to accompany the reading of *Comus* or the *Æneid*. They become domesticated in the heart amidst these propitious shades. But not many bring books under the trees ; nor are they unwise who are contented to translate what silence says. The many-coloured undergraduate lounges there with another of his kind, and may perhaps encounter the shade of some " buck " or "smart " of old, who will set a stamp of antiquity on his glories. Choleric old —— walks there sometimes ; but either a caterpillar falls, or the leaves turn over and unburden themselves of their rain ; and he comes back, loudly thinking that, if a covered cloister had been in the place of the trees, he would not have lost a very ingenious thread of reflection about the greatest good of the greatest number. And —— goes there after a college meeting, and

In a College Garden

changes his mind. The merry breakfaster finds that a turn among the trees will add the button-hole to his complacency. The grave young scholar, with his gown almost to his heels, and the older one whose gown and cap resemble nothing that is worn by any save a tramp, meet there on summer evenings. The freshman gives the highest colour and purest atmosphere to his prophetic imaginings when he walks there first. One says that the garden is partly a confessor and partly an aunt. Above all, it is the resort of those who are about to leave Oxford for ever ; and under its influence those who have forgotten all their ambitions, and those who are beginning to remember them, meet on some June or October afternoon, to decide that it has been worth while ; and between the trees the college has a half-domestic, half-monastic air ; all else is quite shut out, except where, like a curve of smoke, a dome rises, and the wraith of a spire among the clouds.

OLD OXFORD DAYS

CHAPTER VIII

OLD OXFORD DAYS

The history of a college like New or Wadham is written clearly on its walls. It rose by one grand effort, from one grand conception, at the will of founder and architect. All its future uses were more or less plainly implied in the quadrangles, chapel, and hall, through which the opening procession marched with solemn music; they stood in need of little more than time and good fortune. Such a college was then in a sense mature, fully armed and equipped, before the founder's decease.

But it was more characteristic of an Oxford college to be evolved irregularly, by strange and difficult ways, with much sudden expansion and decline, into its present state. Thus Lincoln and Oriel were, for a short time after their foundation, fallow, if not extinct. The latter, in spite of its renovation by a king, after whom it was at first inclined to be named, grew up around the humble, illustrious tenement of La Oriole, where its early scholars dwelt, and whence, they gave their society its lasting name. That cradling tenement has its parallel in many a college history.

In the thirteenth or fourteenth century some Oxford citizen would build a pair of cottages, where a carpenter and an innkeeper came to live. At the inrush of students to welcome a famous lecturer, the spare rooms of those cottages received their share. Some of the lodgers stayed on, liked the carpenter and his wife and family, with whom they lived on terms of social equality; and in a generation the tradition of entertaining scholars was established. A few years saw the formation of a colony of students from one countryside or great estate. As the custom was, they chose a superior from among their number. In those days, if an American had run upstairs to the head, he might have had a more satisfactory answer than he had yesterday to his command : "I've come to take rooms in your college ! " for the hostel was, roughly speaking, an hotel. The members fought side by side in the battles of the nations (viz. Northerners, Southerners, etc.), and of town and gown. They bent over the same books. They sang the same songs. And together they came to love the place, the two cottages and those adjacent into which they had overflowed. Such a group fled from the ancient Brasenose Hall to Stamford, in one of the University migrations, in 1334 ; carried with them the knocker of their lodgings in the shape of a brazen nose, and fixed it to the door of their "Brasenose Hall in Stamford." If they forgot to take it back on their return, it nevertheless "got perched upon the top of the pineal gland " of

the college brain ; and with characteristic spirited piety
the descendants of the old hall-men found it out in
1890, and hung it in a place of honour and safety.

In later life one of the carpenter's tenants became a
bishop, or a royal almoner. Either at the height of
his fame and wealth, or on his deathbed, he would
remember his old retreat, and its associations with law
and Aristotle and

Breed and chese and good ale in a jubbe.

There his old friends or their successors still dwelt,
and learned and taught and fought. So he gave money
for the purchase of the cottages ; a neighbouring garden
plot, perhaps a strip of woodland outside the walls, and
the rents of some home farms for the revenue ; together
with the advowson of a church—if possible the one
which he remembered best in Oxford, or if not, then
one within his diocese or influence. He sketched the
statutes, which fixed the number of the scholars and
the rules for electing new ones and a head. He
himself chose the first head. The scholars were to
remain unmarried and in residence ; to study the Arts,
or Theology, or Canon and Civil Law ; and to pray
for his soul.

The carpenter's and innkeeper's tenants found
themselves suddenly powerful and rich. They had
their own seal, and a new and more settled enthusiasm,
and a diapason of duties and ceremonies, added to their
life. They had their aisle in the church whose shadow
reached them on summer evenings. If their estates were

large and well managed,—if the country was prosperous, and the head obeyed the statutes and the fellows the head, —their progress was swift. Perhaps a legal difficulty interposed delay, or their rents disappeared. Perhaps the fellows quarrelled with the head, or the discipline was such that the fellows climbed into college at late unstatutable hours and became a scandal in the University. But a descendant or neighbour of the founder, or a parishioner of the college living, came to their help. One gave a present, in order that he might be remembered in the college prayers : another sent books : a former fellow who was grateful or pitiful made a rich benefaction when he went to court. Already the little original tenements were tottering or too small. They must build and rebuild. Then a "second founder" adopted as his children that and all succeeding generations of scholars, who should praise him for a benefaction larger than the first.

They pull down the old buildings, all save a flanking wall with a gateway to their taste, and begin to build. The benefactor sends teams of oxen to carry wood and stone. They are quarrying at Eynsham and Headington, and in the benefactor's own distant county. They are felling oaks at Cumnor or Nuneham, actually before the bronzed foliage has crisped to brown. All day the oxen come and go : on the river, the boats are carrying stone, slates, and wood, unless the frost binds the barges among the reeds and the foundation soil breaks the spade. The master mason has already roughly hewn a statue of the patron saint or the founder, or his

rebus and coat of arms. He has decided that the old
doorway shall be the entrance to the college kitchen,
lying far back in the main quadrangle, which will not
only take in the site of the demolished buildings, but
the neighbouring garden and a lane that could be spared.
If he is unfortunate, he may have to stop when he has
completed only the entrance, with the head's lodgings
vigilant above it, and a few sets of rooms adjacent on
either side, already occupied. If all is well, in a few
years, or perhaps at the end of the mason's life, the
shining whole is the admiration of Oxford. The bishop
who is to consecrate the chapel comes informally to see
it a few days beforehand, and is therefore able to
restrain his wonder when he comes pompously with the
chancellor and all the great names of the University.
The chapel and hall face the entrance. All round are
the dwelling rooms, on two storeys, if we count the
long-untenanted attics. On one side alone there is twice
the space of the old cottages ; but the arrangement is
the same—the rooms branching on the left and right
from a staircase that rises from ground to attic. The
library is on a first floor : on one side of it, the
windows invite the earliest light,

> Whan that the belle of laudes gan to rynge
> And freres in the chauncel gonne synge ;

on the other, they enable the late student, who cannot
buy light, to read until the martins cast no shadow as
they pass in June : and there they put the gorgeous
Latin poets and missals, embroidered with colours like

the bank of a brook, and along with them the dull works of a benefactor, in that very corner where the spider loves them to-day. The fellow who loves sleep will not choose the eastward-facing, library side of the quad. But they have made it almost impossible for him to oversleep himself. For in a humbler truckle-bed a younger scholar sleeps near him. Some rooms contain three beds side by side. Leading out of this dormitory are little cupboards or studies, sometimes under lock and key, for solitary work. Most of the walls are ungarnished ; a few are hung with coloured cloth or even frescoed. The furniture is simple and scanty. The hall itself has but a "green hanging of say," a high table for the seniors, and two pairs of forms and tables on trestles for the juniors. The kitchen is more opulent, with its tall andirons, chopping-board, trivet, gridiron, spit, and great pot and chafer of brass, its pans, dishes, and platters ; while in the buttery there are four barrels abroach. Now and then an old member or admirer of the society sends a group of silver vessels : the most honoured becomes the loving cup that circulates on gaudy days ; and with it goes some significant toast, as the *jus suum cuique* at Magdalen accompanies the " Restoration cup," on which the names of James II.'s ejected fellows are engraved. For while the college grows, and sends its just proportion of astute or learned men into the world, it flowers with customs and traditions—prayers in the chapel, festivals in the hall,—the Christmas boar's head decorated with banners at Queen's,—the ancestral vine at Lincoln. At dinner

the tables shine with flagons and tankards, and great
"sprig salts" of silver plate, which were the main college
investment, the pledges of affection, or, as at Wadham,
the customary gift of those who were admitted to the
dignity of the high table. The shining of most was
put out for ever in Charles I.'s melting-pot at New
Inn Hall; and only the lists survive, each tankard and
ewer and candlestick described by its donor's name.

Thus, by the fact of their coming from neighbour
villages and towns, perhaps also from one school, to a
home on which they depended for their learning and
the necessities of life, the fellows and scholars became
knit together, with noticeable characteristics and
peculiarities—almost a family resemblance; and in
religious or political difficulties they made a solid
strength of opinion and influence. A little heresy
might break out under Henry the Eighth or Mary.
A great benefaction might encourage the building of
another quadrangle or a new library, and the institution
of more fellowships and scholarships. They contributed a handsome quantity of plate to the king, and an
officer to his army; or, to a man, resisted the Puritan
intrusion after his death. Such were the more conspicuous events of centuries. The conflicts in the
University, according to some proverbial Latin verses,
were in early times at least as important as the boat
race to-day. They were a subtle measure of the state
of parties and movements; and in these the college
played its part. And when the days of fighting were.
over, there was the University lampoon: "These

paltry scholars," says an old ballad, supposed to be addressed by an Oxford alderman to the Duke of Monmouth,—

> These paltry scholars, blast them with one breath,
> Or they'll rhime your Grace and us to death.

The college was busy in sending out into the world of Church and State its more vigorous members—those who excelled in the age when examinations were disputations that sometimes became almost a form of athletic sport ; and in keeping within its walls the quieter spirits, who were willing to spend a life among manuscripts, in perfecting the management of the college estates, or in the education and discipline of others.   From a scholarship to a fellowship, and from a fellowship to a college living, were frequently made the very calmest windings to a happy decent age, though no doubt the last stage sometimes led to such a regret as this :—

> Why did I sell my College Life
> (He cries) for Benefice and Wife ?
> Return, ye Days ! when endless Pleasure
> I found in Reading or in Leisure !
> When calm around the Common Room
> I puff'd my daily Pipe's Perfume !
> Rode for a stomach, and inspected,
> At Annual Bottlings, corks selected :
> And din'd untax'd, untroubled, under
> The Portrait of our pious Founder !

It was a fine thing to sit day after day, in rooms sweetened, as in Burton's day, with juniper, or in the college library, which was as a bay or river mouth leading into the very land of silence—to sit and write, or not write, as you pleased ; and, in the days when books were no longer shelved with their faces to the wall, look up at

Bullarium
Cherubini

printed in gold upon the glowing calf, and making mystical combinations as night came on. There, and in hall, chapel, study, and garden, men doomed to very diverse fates and stations went and still go, and found it possible to live a more enchanted life than anywhere else.

The refractory Headington stone crumbled, and while the classical buildings became yearly less handsome than when the masons left them, the Gothic gained by the rich inlay and delicate waste of weather and time. As if time and weather wrote the chronicles of the society, the walls came to have a singular influence upon each generation, and gave them, as it were, a common ancestry and blood—noble blood, for all. Even when they departed they had the irrefragable right of exiles to look back and salute.

And yet how different the life within those walls which some now living can remember! Sixty years ago, they lament, "no man was ever seen in the streets of Oxford after lunch without being dressed as he would have been in Pall Mall." Charles Reade at Magdalen "created a panic even among the junior members" by wearing a green coat and brass buttons, as Dean of Arts. Sixty years before that, George Colman had matriculated in a grass-green coat, "with the furiously bepowdered pate of an ultra coxcomb." And now, says the first-quoted authority, "shooting-jackets of all patterns, in which it is not given to every man to look like a gentleman," have taken the place of frock-coat, tall hat, and gloves, "in which every one looked well." The change from knee-breeches to trousers early last century was made possible by the gross lenience of a proctor.

Without college or university games, the old Oxford day was very much unlike our own. Bonfires of celebration, almost alone among modern amusements, are of great antiquity, in street and quad. A hundred years ago the man who would now row or play cricket for his college, was hunting, or pole-jumping across the fields; or, if he was original, he took the long walks which were popular a few generations ago, but are now so exceptional that I know nobody who ever saw, and recognised, Matthew Arnold's tree, though some are lazily inclined to believe that it is the one elm that dwells with the seven firs on Cumnor Hurst.

One of the few college games was confined to the fives courts, which lay within the walls and have long disappeared, and are inconceivable to-day, when competition and spectators on ground remote from the colleges are characteristic of Oxford sport. Earlier still, a form of college game was the "vile and horrid sport" of forcibly shaving those who were about to become Masters of Arts, and the "tucking" (*i.e.* scratching on the chin with the thumb nail) of freshmen, which the first Earl of Shaftesbury put down at Exeter. These customs cast but a feeble shadow to-day in the occasional solemnity of trimming a contemporary's

exuberant or ill-kept hair. A more appropriate form
of celebrating the taking of degrees was an elaborate
supper, which is now less often possible, when a man
frequently takes his degree in solitude and leaves
Oxford immediately. William Paston, in the fifteenth
century, writes, that he was made bachelor on a Friday
and had his feast on the Monday following. He was
promised a gift of venison, and though disappointed,
his guests "were pleased with such meat as they had."
Even William of Wykeham, who forbade every possible
game to his scholars at New College, and would not
allow the post-prandial leisure to be spent on ordinary
days around the fire in the middle of his great hall, provided that, after supper, "on festivals and other winter
nights, on which, in honour of God, his Mother, or
some other saint," there is a fire in the hall, the
fellows might indulge in singing or reading "poems,
chronicles of the realm, and the wonders of the world."
Some of the college halls preserved their old central
fireplaces, under a louvre, until early in the last century.
While the fellows dined, a servitor stood there, and
read aloud from the Bible, in the first days of the
college ; or, as at Trinity in 1792, recited a passage
from Homer or Virgil or Milton. Southey records it
as a rule, that every member of the University could
go by right once a year to Balliol hall, and " be treated
with bread and cheese and beer, and all on condition
that, when called upon, he should either sing a song
or tell a story." Those who were unqualified doubtless stayed away. Yet there is little sign that the

temperate or secluded undergraduate suffered for his gifts. Whitefield himself, who cost his relatives £24 for his first three years, and wore "woollen gloves, a patched gown, and dirty shoes," says that the other men left him alone when "he became better than other people," as a "singular odd fellow," at Pembroke. There was, however, one custom which must have left such men with a sore memory. For the "fresh night" was long the common doom of men soon after entering the University. There were fires of charcoal in the hall on All Saints' eve, All Saints' day and night, and onwards to Christmas day and Candlemas day; and the freshmen were brought in before an assembly of their seniors among the undergraduates. Anthony à Wood describes the ordeal thus :—

"On Candlemas day, or before, every freshman had warning given him to provide his speech, to be spoken in the public hall before the undergraduates and servants on Shrove Tuesday night that followed, being always the time for the observation of that ceremony.

"Feb. 15, 164$\frac{7}{8}$, Shrove Tuesday, the fire being made in the common hall before five of the clock at night, the fellows would go to supper before six, and making an end sooner than at other times, they left the hall to the liberty of the undergraduates, but with an admonition from one of the fellows (who was then principal of the undergraduates and postmasters [at Merton]) that all things should be carried in good order. While they were at supper in the hall, the cook (Will Noble) was making the lesser of the brass pots full of cawdel at the

freshmen's charge ; which, after the hall was free from
the fellows, was brought up and set before the fire in
the said hall.   Afterwards every freshman, according
to seniority, was to pluck off his gown and band, and
if possible make himself look like a scoundrel.   This
done, they were conducted each after the other to the
high table, and there made to stand on a form placed
thereon : from whence they were to speak their speech
with an audible voice to the company ; which if well
done, the person that spoke it was to have a cup of
caudle and no salted drink ; if indifferently, some
caudle and some salted drink ; but if dull, nothing was
given to him but salted drink, or salt put in college
beer, with tucks to boot.   Afterwards when they were
to be admitted into the fraternity, the senior cook was
to administer to them an oath over an old shoe.   After
which, spoken with gravity, the freshman kissed the
shoe, put on his gown and band, and took his place
among the seniors."

Wood himself not only earned pure caudle, but sack
as well, with an oration in this vein :—

" Most reverend Seniors,—May it please your
Gravities to admit into your presence a kitten of the
Muses, and a meer frog of Helicon to croak the
cataracts of his plumbeous cerebrosity before your
sagacious ingenuities.   I am none of the University
blood-hounds that seek for preferment, and whose
noses are as acute as their ears, that lie perdue for
places, and who, good saints ! do groan till *the Visitation* comes.   These are they that esteem a tavern as

bad as purgatory, and wine more superstitious than holy water ; and therefore I hope this honourable convocation will not suffer one of that tribe to taste of the sack, lest they should be troubled with a vertigo and their heads turn *round*."

Except at such a special season as that, the old Oxford day bore more resemblance than our own to the life elsewhere. The fashions in cards and dress were the same as in London ; the outdoor amusements were those of other town or country gentlemen. There was horse-racing at Spurton Hill and Brackley, cock-fighting at Holywell. Edgeworth's contemporaries attended the assizes, and interfered on behalf of justice, in spite of sheriff and judge. Anthony à Wood went to fish at Wheatley Bridge, and "nutted at Shotover by the way." And early rising was a tradition in every college until last century. The undergraduate, who to-day lives on historical principles, is often later than his sixteenth-century original was to dine, when he sits at his breakfast of steak and XX in a fine old room. Chapel at six o'clock and a lecture at seven was a common doom. Shelley and Hogg, after their days spent in shooting at a mark, and making ducks and drakes and paper boats at a Shotover pond, sat up, indeed, until two, over their conversations on literature and chemistry, but rose at seven, because it was customary. While dinner was at ten or eleven, breakfast was an informal meal. Some attempted to do without it : hence a morning preacher swooned on the altar steps. Wood speaks of the juniors "at breakfast in hall " in

Old Oxford Days

1661. The majority took beer and bread from the buttery, and probably taking it in one another's rooms, started the genial custom of breakfast parties, which was perfected early in the nineteenth century. "Let the tender swain," says the well-spiced *Oxford Sausage*, a mid-eighteenth-century product of Oxford (and Cambridge) wits,—

> Let the tender Swain
> Each Morn regale on nerve-relaxing Tea,
> Companion meet of languor-loving Nymph :
> Be mine each Morn with eager appetite
> And Hunger undissembled, to repair
> To friendly Buttery; there on smoking Crust
> And foaming Ale to banquet unrestrained,
> Material Breakfast!   Thus in ancient Days
> Our ancestors robust with liberal cups
> Usher'd the Morn, unlike the squeamish Sons
> Of modern Times : Nor ever had the Might
> Of Britons brave decay'd, had thus they fed,
> With British Ale improving British worth.

The institution of breakfast, whatever happened to British worth, was certainly helped forward by the tea, rolls, and toast which slowly ousted ale. Lectures and disputations in private or in the Schools followed breakfast. The latter possibly encouraged intercollegiate sports, since Exeter and Christ Church on one occasion resolved their disputation into a fight which attracted Masters of Arts. And well it might ; for otherwise they were in danger of dining like fighting cocks and amusing themselves like doves : the sixteenth-century fellows of Corpus, for example, were permitted no games but ball in the college garden. Examinations are still a select and expensive form of amusement.

Oxford

The stories told of celebrated men and their *viva voce* conflicts with examiners, and the like, have inspired more than one to go into the Schools in a mood of smiling irreverence. The fame resulting, it is true, has to be propagated by much anecdote from the lips of the hero himself. In the Middle Ages the humour was of a lustier kind. The parsley crown went, or should have gone, to the most brazen giver and taker of learned wit. In Anthony à Wood's day, one William George, " cynical and hirsute in his behaviour," was a noted sophister and disputant, and improved his purse by preparing the exercises of the dull or lazy for public recitation. The nature of these examinations, in their dull old age, has been recorded by one who took part :—

" Two boys, or men, as they call themselves, agree to *do generals* together. The first stage in this mighty work is to produce arguments. These are always handed down from generation to generation, on long slips of paper, and consist of foolish syllogisms on foolish subjects. The next step is to go for a *liceat* to one of the petty officers, called the Regent Master of the Schools, who subscribes his name to the questions, and receives sixpence as his fee. When the important day arrives, the two doubty disputants go into a large dusty room, full of dirt and cobwebs, with walls and wainscot decorated with the names of former disputants, who, to divert the tedious hours, cut out their names with their penknives or wrote verses with a pencil. Here they sit in mean desks, opposite to each other, from one till three. Not once in a hundred times does

236

any officer enter ; and if he does, he hears one syllogism or two, and then makes a bow, and departs, as he came and remained, in solemn silence. The disputants then return to the amusement of cutting the desks, carving their names, or reading Sterne's *Sentimental Journey*, or some other edifying novel."

Thus, towards the end of the eighteenth century, " great progress is made towards the wished-for honour of a bachelor's degree " ; the goal might be reached, if the undergraduate knew a few " jolly young Masters of Arts," by answering questions concerning the pedigree of a race-horse. Such was the lack of interest in the disputations that they were called " wall " lectures, after the name of their principal auditor.

A little poaching gave a very attractive substitute for cross-country running. But increasing college discipline and the heightening average of wealth and birth among students cut off the more violent sports of the Middle Ages. The unattached, poor Welsh and Irish students, who kept up the University name for rough and adventurous relaxations, disappeared before the Reformation ; and after the Poor Law Act of 1531 had condemned begging scholars, who were not authorised under the seal of a university, to be treated as able-bodied beggars, there can have been few to poach at Shotover and Abingdon. The masked Mohock revels and Jacobite struttings of the Augustan age were a poor alternative. The blithe and fearless spirit of trespassing, so common among undergraduates, is the sole survival to-day, if we exclude the pious uprooting

Oxford

of stakes and fences on fields supposed (by reference to Doomsday Book) to be common land. Before and after the Puritans, who preferred music in their rooms, there was free access to the acting of dramas in Latin and English, and earlier still, to the miracle plays of Herod and Noah and the like. Even during the Commonwealth private theatricals were popular; and Wood speaks of one John Glendall, a fellow of Brasenose, who was the witty *terræ filius* in 1658, when the Acts were kept in St. Mary's Church, as "a great mimick, and acted well in several plays which the scholars acted by stealth in Kettle Hall, the refectory at Gloster Hall," etc.

For centuries the ale-houses were full of university life. At one time there were three hundred in Oxford. They had excellent uses before a common room perfected the homeliness of the college; and even afterwards, in the eighteenth century, a poetical club met at "The Tuns" to display their wit. There the undergraduates freshened and shared their wit, before each had an ample sitting-room, and before the junior common room,—where now the newspaper rustles, and the debate roars or chirps, and the senior scholar, on rare occasions, speaks to a not wholly reverent college meeting from the time-honoured elevation of the mantelpiece. The men of Balliol continued the old-fashioned devotion to the "Split Crow" in Broad Street long after the coffee-house had become fashionable. The vice-chancellor, being president of the rival and neighbouring society of Trinity, scoffed at the Master's attempt to discourage them; "so now they may be sots by authority." The disorder was winked at because it increased the "natural stupidity" of the Balliol men of the day. But the attitude of the University towards humour two centuries ago was a wily mixture of patronage and ferocity. The *terræ filius* was only not official in his reckless bombardment of order and authority at the annual University Act. It was as though a jackdaw should be invited to church. He and his companion (for they hunted in couples) were chosen, as regularly as proctors, by election; and to become *terræ filius* must have been the blue riband of the wilder sort of University wits. Year after year pairs of *terræ filii* fired their random shots at great and small, always with audacity, sometimes with the utmost scurrility; and year after year one or both of the pair suffered expulsion, or, like Addison's father, public humiliation, for their scandalous and opprobrious words, which no doubt earned the gratitude of irresponsible juniors.

It was long a common recreation, a recreation only, to go on the river in a boat, and to row or be rowed to some place of meditation or festivity, or to go with music and wine upon the Isis to Godstow Bridge or Sandford—

> And there
> Beckley provides accustom'd fare
> Of eels, and perch, and brown beefsteak.

And the mention of Sandford carries with it many memories for modern Oxford men, even if perch is not always to be had—of winter afternoons when the mulled port was as sweet as a carnation, and a voice from a slowly-gliding barge was the sole sound in all the land. One joyous company long ago went, "like country fiddlers," to Farringdon fair, with cithern, bass viol, and violin. The city itself offered other amusements than the theatre, music hall, billiard tables, and picture shows of to-day. Freaks, monstrosities, mountebanks, jugglers, were welcome not only to undergraduates of fifteen or sixteen. There was "a brazen head that could speak and answer" at the Fleur de Lace on one day; on another, strange beasts. On May-day a maypole stood near St. Peter's-in-the-East and opposite the "Mitre." A bear-baiting was always a possibility. There was a fencing school at hand. One who cared for none of these has left this account of his Oxford day in the seventeenth century :—

> *Morn, mend hose, stu. Greek, breakfast, Austen, quoque dinner;*
> *Afternoon, wa. me., cra. nu., take a cup, quoque supper—*

i.e., interprets Wood, in the morning he mended his stockings, studied Greek, took breakfast, studied St. Augustine, and dined; and in the afternoon, walked in Christ Church meadows, cracked nuts, took a drink, and had supper.

Above all, in and after the time of Cromwell the city provided coffee-houses,—the real, steaming, smoking, witty thing. The hospitality and spirit of careless intercourse between college and college which they fostered belong to the present day. They were first opened, too, at a time when much of mediæval life was

Old Oxford Days

departing, when Christmas sports were dying, and Latin conversation at dinner and supper was going out of use ; and Anthony à Wood laments that scholar-like conversation (" viz. by quoting the fathers, producing an antient verse from the poets suitable to his discourse ") was accounted pedantic, and " nothing but news and the affairs of Christendom," he says scornfully, " is discoursed of, and that generally at coffee-houses." At some, perhaps at all of them, there was a light library, which apparently resembled the library of a modern college barge. A copy of Rabelais, with poems and plays, all chained in the old manner, embellished Short's coffee-house. Later came the *Tatlers* and *Spectators* and *Connoisseurs*, for " such as have neglected or lost their Latin or Greek," as Tom Warton said :—

" As there are here books suited to every Taste, so there are liquors adapted to every species of reading. Amorous tales may be perused over Arrack punch and jellies ; insipid odes over orgeat or capilaire ; politics over coffee ; divinity over port ; and defences of bad generals and bad ministers over whipt syllabubs. In a word, in these libraries instruction and pleasure go hand in hand ; and we may pronounce, in a literal sense, that learning remains no longer a dry pursuit." And in Gibbon's day the dons changed their seats from chapel to hall, and from common room to coffee-house, in an indolent circle ; and not only dons, but the infinite variety of University types in the distinguishing raiment of that day—

241

Oxford

Such nice distinction one perceives
In cut of gown, and hoods and sleeves,
Marking degrees, or style, or station,
Of Members free, or on foundation,
That were old Cato here narrator
He must perforce have nomenclator.

There, or at an ale-house, which appears to have been
less exposed to a proctorial raid, the sociable spent the
Oxford evening, which grew longer as the nineteenth
century approached. Sunday evenings were frequently
devoted to the fair sex in Merton walks, which were
always gay.

My hair in wires exact and nice,
I'll trim my cap to smallest size,
That *Polly* sure may see me,

exclaims an eighteenth-century spark, with a hint that
the kindly relations between town and gown sometimes
reached the married state. Yet another writer with an
eye for the amusing side of Oxford life drew the
following picture, which a diligent seeker might, with
difficulty, parallel to-day. Gainlove and Ape-all, two
Oxford undergraduates, are talking :—

" *Gainlove*. What, bound for the Port of Wedlock,
Sir ?

" *Ape-all*. No, no, no, no, Sir ; I only use her as a
Pleasure boat to dabble about the stream with, purely
for a Passo Tempo, or so. O Lord, Sir, I have been
at London, and know more of the world than to make
love to a woman I intend to marry—only it diverts the
spleen to talk to a girl sometimes, you know—and 'tis
such a comedy, when one gallants them to college, to

Old Oxford Days

see all the young Fellows froze with envy, stand centinel in their niches, like the figures of the Kings round the Royal Exchange. And the old Dons who would take no more notice of one at another time than a bishop of a country curate, will come cringing, cap in hand, to offer to show the ladies the curiosities of the College— when the duce knows they only want to be nibbling."

Those who liked not these things had at least as good an opportunity of quiet work as to-day. A separate set of rooms for each member of a college had gradually become almost universal in the eighteenth century ; and the great outer door or "oak" shut off those who wished from the rest of the world. Shelley was so pleased with that impervious door that he exclaimed : the oak "is surely the tree of knowledge!" The simplicity of the quarters within, before much of undergraduate social life was passed in their rooms, would astonish modern eyes, if we may judge from contemporary cuts, that show a few chairs, a small table with central leg, a cap and gown on the wall; an inkhorn hanging by the window, a pair of bellows and tongs by the fire, and over the mantel-piece a picture or mirror. But there the undergraduate was safe from duns "with vocal heel thrice thundering at the gate," and, let us hope, from dons, in colleges where they came round at nine in the evening, to see that he kept good hours. Dibdin tells us that, as he closed the *Curiosities of Literature*, he saw the Gothic battlements outside his window "streaked with the dapple light of morning." Ten years later, in the first year

THE OXFORD COUNTRY

Oxford

I could wish that an inexorable Five Mile Act had kept it clear of red brick. Newman and Ruskin hinted at the same. I know not how to describe the spirit which turns a few miles of peaceful southern country into something so unique. But if I mention a wood or a stream, let the reader paint in, as it were, something sweet and shadowy in the distance, with his imagination or recollection; let it be as some subtle perfume in a *pot pourri* which makes it different from all others.

There is a beautiful, sloping acre, not far from Oxford, which a number of great elms divide into aisles and nave, while at one end a curving hawthorn and maple hedge completes them with an apse. Towards Oxford, the space is almost shut in by remote elms. On one side I hear the soft and sibilant fall of soaking grass before the scythe. The rain and sun alternating are like two lovers in dialogue; the rain smiles from the hills when the sun shines, and the sun also while the rain is falling. When the rain is not over and the sun has interrupted, the nightingale sings, where the stitch-wort is starry amidst long grass that bathes the sweep-ing branches of thorn and brier; and I am now stabbed, and now caressed, by its changing song. Through the elms on either side, hot, rank grasses rise, crowned with a vapour of parsley flowers. A white steam from the soil faintly mists the grass at intervals. The grass and elms seem to be suffering in the rain, suffering for their quietness and solitude, to be longing for something, as perhaps Eden also dropped "some natural tears" when left a void. A potent, warm, and not quite soothing

The Oxford Country

perfume creeps over the grass, and makes the May blossom something elvish. I turn and look east. Almost at once, all these things are happily composed into one pleasant sense, and are but a frame to a tower and three spires of Oxford, like clouds—but the sky is suddenly cloudless.

I suppose that ivy has the same graceful ways on all old masonry, yet I have caught myself remembering, as if it were unique, that perfect ancient ivy that makes an arcade of green along the wall of Godstow nunnery. And in the same way, above all others I remember the pollard willows that lean this way and that along the Oxford streams—like prehistoric sculpture in winter, but in summer a green wave and full of voices. Never have I seen sunsets like those which make Wytham Wood and Marley Wood great purple clouds, and the clouds overhead more solid than they. How pleasant are Cherwell and Evenlode, and those angry little waters at Ferry Hinksey! When I see the rain a white cloud and Shotover Hill a grey cloud, I seem never before to have seen the sweetness of rain. October is nowhere so much itself as among the Hinksey elms, when the fallen leaves smell of tea (and who that loves tea and autumn will cast a stone?). The trees, whether they stand alone or in societies, are most perfect in autumn. Something in the soil or climate preserves their farewell hues as in a protracted sunset. Looking at them at nightfall, it is hard to believe that they have been amidst ten thousand sunsets and remained the same; for they ponder great matters, and not only in the autumn, but in May, when the silence is startled by the gurgling laughter of the hen cuckoo. When spring comes into the land, I remember a mulberry that suspended its white blossom, among black boughs, over a shining lawn at the edge of the city; and the bells that in March or April seemed to be in league with spring, as we heard them from the fields. And how well a conversation would grow and blossom between Headington and Wheatley or Osney and Eaton! Some that loved not the country would flourish strangely in wisdom or folly as the roads rose or fell, or as the grey oak stems of Bagley Wood began to make a mist around us. The only incidents, in twenty miles, were the occasional sprints of one who was devoted to a liver, or the cometary passing of one on a bicycle that sang *Le Roi d'Ivetot* as if it were a psalm containing the whole duty of man. And how a book —even a "schools" book —taken on the river or the hills, would yield a great sweetness to alternate hand-lings and laughter of several companions; or, if it were a dull book, might be made to yield more than its author ever meant. I have ever thought that the churchyard with a broken cross at Hinksey, and the willows below and the elms above, if one takes George Herbert there, is a better argument for the Church than Jewel and Chillingworth, if the old yew had not seemed the priest of some old superstition still powerful.

No one can walk much in the Oxford country without becoming a Pantheist. The influence of the city, the memories, the books he is fresh from, help the indolent

walker, who is content to sit under a hedge and wait
for the best things, to make his gods. The lanes are
peopled with no fairies such as in Wales and Ireland
nimbly feed the fantasy, which here, in consequence, is
apt to take flight in wonderful ways. I remember one
(and Ovid was not at all in his mind) who was all but
confident that he saw Persephone on flat pastures and
red ploughlands, gleaming between green trees, when
the hawthorn was not yet over and the roses had begun,
and the sapphire dragon-fly was afloat, on the Cherwell,
as the boat made a cool sound among the river's hair,
betwixt Water Eaton and Islip. On the quiet, misty,
autumn mornings, the hum of threshing machines was
solemn ; and there at least it was a true harmony of
autumn, and the man casting sheaves from the rick
was exalted—

> Neque illum
> Flava Ceres alto nequiquam spectat Olympo.

Everywhere the fancy, unaided by earlier fancies, sets
to work very busily in these fields. I have on several
afternoons gone some way towards the beginning of
a new mythology, which might in a thousand years
puzzle the Germans. The shadowy, half-apprehended
faces of new deities float before my eyes, and I have
wondered whether Apollo and Diana are not immortal
presences wheresoever there are awful trees and alternating spaces of cool or sunlit lawn. . . . In the lanes
there seems to be another religion for the night.
There is a fitful wind, and so slow that as we walk we

can follow its path while it shakes the heavy leaves and dewy grass; and we feel as if we were trespassing on holy ground; the land seems to have changed masters, or rather to have One. Often I saw a clean-limbed beech, pale and slender, yet firm in its loftiness, that shook delicately arched branches at the top, and below held out an arm on which a form of schoolboys might have sat,—rising out of fine grass and printing its perfect outlines on the sky,—and I could fancy it enjoyed a life of pleasure that was health, beauty that was strength, thought that was repose.

The Oxford country is rich in footpaths, as any one will know that goes the round from Folly Bridge, through South Hinksey, to the "Fox" at Boar's Hill (where the scent of wallflower and hawthorn comes in through the window with the sound of the rain and the nightingale); and then away, skirting Wootton and Cumnor, past the "Bear" (with its cool flagged room looking on a field of gold, and Cumnor Church tower among elms); and back over the Hurst, where he turns, under the seven firs and solitary elm, to ponder the long, alluring view towards Stanton Harcourt and Bablock Hythe. He may take that walk many times, or wish to take it, and yet never touch the same footpaths; and never be sure of the waste patch of bluebell and furze, haunted by linnet and whinchat; the newly harrowed field, where the stones shine like ivory after rain; the green lane, where the beech leaves lie in February, and rise out of the snow, untouched by it, in polished amber; the orchard, where the grass is gloomy in April with the shadow of bright cherry flowers.

One such footpath I remember, that could be seen falling among woods and rising over hills, faint and winding, and disappearing at last,—like a vision of the perfect quiet life. We started once along it, over one of the many fair little Oxford bridges, one that cleared the stream in three graceful leaps of arching stone. The hills were cloudy with woods in the heat. On either hand, at long distances apart, lay little grey houses under scalloped capes of thatch, and here and there white houses, like children of that sweet land— *albi circum ubera nati*. For the most part we saw only the great hawthorn hedge, which gave us the sense of a companion always abreast of us, yet always cool and fresh as if just setting out. It was cooler when a red-hot bicyclist passed by. A sombre river, noiselessly sauntering seaward, far away dropped with a murmur, among leaves, into a pool. That sound alone made tremble the glassy dome of silence that extended miles on miles. All things were lightly powdered with gold, by a lustre that seemed to have been sifted through gauze. The hazy sky, striving to be blue, was reflected as purple in the waters. There, too, sunken and motionless, lay amber willow leaves ; some floated down. Between the sailing leaves, against the false sky, hung the willow shadows,—shadows of willows overhead, with waving foliage, like the train of a bird of paradise. Everywhere the languid perfumes of corruption. Brown leaves laid their fingers on the cheek as they fell; and here and there the hoary reverse of a willow leaf gleamed in the crannied bases of the trees. A plough, planted in mid-field, was curved like the wings of a bird alighting.

We could not walk as slowly as the river flowed; yet that seemed the true pace to move in life, and so reach the great grey sea. Hand in hand with the river wound the path, until twilight began to drive her dusky flocks across the west, and a light wind knitted the aspen branches against a silver sky with a crescent moon, as, troubled tenderly by autumnal maladies of soul, we came to our place of rest,—a grey, immemorial house with innumerable windows.

IN PRAISE OF OXFORD

CHAPTER X

MANY have written in praise of Oxford, and so finely that I have made this selection with difficulty. I have excluded the work of living men, because I am not familiar with it. Among that which is included will be found passages from the writings of one who was at both Universities, John Lyly ; of two who were at Cambridge only, Dryden and Wordsworth ; of two who were at neither, Hazlitt and Hawthorne ; and of several brilliant lovers of Oxford whose faith was filial and undivided. Almost all the quotations have wit or beauty enough to defend them, even had they been less apposite : their charm is redoubled in this place, since they are in Oxford's praise. They are worthy of a city which a learned German compares with the creations of Poussin and Claude. But they are in no need of compliment. I could only wish that I had put down nothing unworthy of their blessing. I have ; and so they stand in place of epilogue, where they perform the not unprecedented duty of apology.

257

Oxford

" There are also in this Islande two famous Universities, the one *Oxford*, the other *Cambridge*, both for the profession of all sciences, for Divinitie, phisicke, Lawe, and for all kinde of learning, excelling all the Universities of Christendome.

" I was myself in either of them, and like them both so well, that I meane not in the way of controversie to preferre any for the better in Englande, but both for the best in the world, saving this, that Colledges in *Oxenford* are much stately for the building, and *Cambridge* much more sumptuous for the houses in the towne, but the learning neither lyeth in the free stones of the one, nor the fine streates of the other, for out of them both do dayly proceede men of great wisdome, to rule in the common welth, of learning to instruct the Common people, of all singuler kinde of professions to do good to all. And let this suffice, not to enquire which of them is the superior, but that neither of them have their equall, neither to ask which of them is the most auncient, but whether any other bee so famous."

JOHN LYLY.

" Where the Cherwell flows along with the Isis, and their divided streams make several little sweet and pleasant islands, is seated on a rising vale the most famous University of Oxford, in Saxon Oxenford, our most noble Athens, the seat of the English Muses, the prop and pillar, nay the sun, the eye, the very soul of the nation : the most celebrated fountain of wisdom and learning, from whence Religion, Letters and Good

In Praise of Oxford

Manners, are happily diffused thro' the whole Kingdom. A delicate and most beautiful city, whether we respect the neatness of private buildings, or the stateliness of public structures, or the healthy and pleasant situation. For the plain on which it stands is walled in, as it were, with hills of wood, which keeping out on one side the pestilential south wind, on the other, the tempestuous west, admit only the purifying east, and the north that disperses all unwholesome vapours. From which delightful situation, Authors tell us it was heretofore call'd *Bellositum*."—CAMDEN.

Ye sacred Nurseries of blooming Youth !
In whose collegiate shelter England's Flowers
Expand, enjoying through their vernal hours
The air of liberty, the light of truth ;
Much have ye suffered from Time's gnawing tooth :
Yet, O ye spires of Oxford ! domes and towers !
Gardens and groves ! your presence overpowers
The soberness of reason ; till, in sooth,
Transformed, and rushing on a bold exchange
I slight my own beloved Cam, to range
Where silver Isis leads my stripling feet ;
Pace the long avenue, or glide adown
The stream-like windings of that glorious street—
An eager Novice robed in fluttering gown !
WORDSWORTH.

"King James, 1605, when he came to our University of Oxford, and, amongst other edifices, now went to view that famous Library, renewed by Sir Thomas Bodley, in imitation of Alexander, at his departure brake out into that noble speech, If I were not a King, I would be an University man : and if it were

259

so that I must be a prisoner, if I might have my wish, I would desire to have no other prison than that Library, and to be chained together with so many good Authors *et mortuis magistris*. So sweet is the delight of study, the more learning they have (as he that hath a Dropsy, the more he drinks the thirstier he is), the more they covet to learn, and the last day is *prioris discipulus*; harsh at first learning is, *radices amaræ*, but *fructus dulces*, according to that of Isocrates, pleasant at last; the longer they live, the more they are enamoured of the Muses. *Heinsius*, the keeper of the Library at Leyden in Holland, was mewed up in it all the year long; and that which to my thinking should have bred a loathing caused in him a greater liking. *I no sooner* (saith he) *come into the Library, but I bolt the door to me, excluding lust, ambition, avarice, and all such vices, whose nurse is idleness, the mother of ignorance, and Melancholy herself; in the very lap of eternity, amongst so many divine souls, I take my seat, with so lofty a spirit and sweet content, that I pity all our great ones, and rich men that know not this happiness.*"

The Anatomy of Melancholy.

But by the sacred genius of this place,
By every Muse, by each domestic grace,
Be kind to wit, which but endeavours well,
And, where you judge, presumes not to excel.
Our poets hither for adoption come,
As nations sued to be made free of Rome :
Not in the suffragating tribes to stand,
But in your utmost, last, provincial band.
If his ambition may those hopes pursue,
Who with religion loves your arts and you,

In Praise of Oxford

Oxford to him a dearer name shall be,
Than his own mother university.
Thebes did his green unknowing youth engage,
He chooses Athens in his riper age.

DRYDEN.

" Rome has been called the ' Sacred City '—might not *our* Oxford be called so too ?   There is an air about it, resonant of joy and hope : it speaks with a thousand tongues to the heart : it weaves its mighty shadow over the imagination : it stands in lowly sublimity, on the 'hill of ages,' and points with prophetic fingers to the sky: it greets the eager gaze from afar, 'with glistening spires and pinnacles adorned,' that shine with an eternal light as with the lustre of setting suns ; and a dream and a glory hover round its head, as the spirits of former times, a throng of intellectual shapes, are seen retreating or advancing to the eye of memory : its streets are paved with the names of learning that can never wear out : its green quadrangles breathe the silence of thought, conscious of the weight of yearnings innumerable after the past, of loftiest aspirations for the future : Isis babbles of the Muse, its waters are from the springs of Helicon, its Christ Church meadows, classic, Elysian fields !—We could pass our lives in Oxford without having or wanting any other idea— that of the place is enough.   We imbibe the air of thought ; we stand in the presence of learning.   We are admitted into the Temple of Fame, we feel that we are in the Sanctuary, on holy ground, and 'hold high converse with the mighty dead.'   The enlightened and

Oxford

the ignorant are on a level, if they have but faith in the tutelary genius of the place. We may be wise by proxy, and studious by prescription. Time has taken upon himself the labour of thinking ; and accumulated libraries leave us leisure to be dull. There is no occasion to examine the buildings, the churches, the colleges, by the rules of architecture, to reckon up the streets to compare it with Cambridge (Cambridge lies out of the way, on one side of the world)—but woe to him who does not feel in passing through Oxford that he is in 'no mean city,' that he is surrounded with the monuments and lordly mansions of the mind of man, outvying in pomp and splendour the courts and palaces of princes, rising like an exhalation in the night of ignorance, and triumphing over barbaric foes, saying, 'All eyes shall see me, and all knees shall bow to me !' —as the shrine where successive ages came to pay their pious vows, and slake the sacred thirst of knowledge, where youthful hopes (an endless flight) soared to truth and good, and where the retired and lonely student brooded over the historic, or over fancy's page, imposing high tasks for himself, framing high destinies for the race of man—the lamp, the mine, the well-head whence the spark of learning was kindled, its stream flowed, its treasures were spread out through the remotest corners of the land and to distant nations. Let him who is fond of indulging a dream-like existence go to Oxford, and stay there ; let him study this magnificent spectacle, the same under all aspects, with the mental twilight tempering the glare of noon, or

In Praise of Oxford

mellowing the silver moonlight ; let him not catch the
din of scholars or teachers, or dine or sup with them,
or speak a word to any of its privileged inhabitants ;
for if he does, the spell will be broken, the poetry and
the religion gone, and the palace of enchantment will
melt from his embrace into thin air ! ”

HAZLITT.

“ Oxford . . . must remain its own sole expression ;
and those whose sad fortune it may be never to behold
it have no better resource than to dream about grey,
weather-stained, ivy-grown edifices, wrought with
quaint Gothic ornament, and standing around grassy
quadrangles, where cloistered walks have echoed to the
quiet footsteps of twenty generations, — lawns and
gardens of luxurious repose, shadowed with canopies of
foliage, and lit up with sunny glimpses through arch-
ways of great boughs, — spires, towers, and turrets, each
with its history and legend, — dimly magnificent chapels,
with painted windows of rare beauty and brilliantly
diversified hues, creating an atmosphere of richest
gloom, — vast college halls, high-windowed, oaken-
panelled, and hung around with portraits of the men
in every age whom the University has nurtured to be
illustrious, — long vistas of alcoved libraries, where the
wisdom and learned folly of all time is shelved, —
kitchens (we throw in this feature by way of ballast,
and because it would not be English Oxford without
its beef and beer) with huge fireplaces, capable of
roasting a hundred joints at once, — and cavernous

Oxford

cellars, where rows of piled-up hogsheads seethe and
fume with that mighty malt-liquor which is the true
milk of Alma Mater: make all these things vivid in
your dream, and you will never know nor believe how
inadequate is the result to represent even the merest
outside of Oxford."—HAWTHORNE.

"Beautiful city! so venerable, so lovely, so un-
ravaged by the fierce intellectual life of our century, so
serene!

There are our young barbarians, all at play!

And yet steeped in sentiment as she lies, spreading her
gardens to the moonlight, and whispering from her
towers the last enchantments of the Middle Age, who
will deny that Oxford, by her ineffable charm, keeps
ever calling us nearer to the true goal of all of us, to
the ideal, to perfection,—to beauty, in a word, which is
only truth seen from another side?—nearer, perhaps,
than all the science of Tübingen. Adorable dreamer,
whose heart has been so romantic! who hast given
thyself so prodigally, given thyself to sides and to
heroes not mine, only never to the Philistines! home
of lost causes, and forsaken beliefs, and unpopular
names, and impossible loyalties! whose example could
ever so inspire us to keep down the Philistine in ourselves, what teacher could ever so save us from that
bondage to which we are all so prone, that bondage
which Goethe, in his incomparable lines on the death of
Schiller, makes it his friend's highest praise (and nobly
did Schiller deserve the praise) to have left miles out of

264

sight behind him—the bondage of *Was uns alle bändigt*, DAS GEMEINE! She will forgive me, even if I have unwittingly drawn upon her a shot or two aimed at her unworthy son; for she is generous, and the cause in which I fight is, after all, hers. Apparitions of a day, what is our puny warfare against the Philistines, compared with the warfare which this queen of romance has been waging against them for centuries, and will wage after we are gone?"

MATTHEW ARNOLD.

INDEX

Index